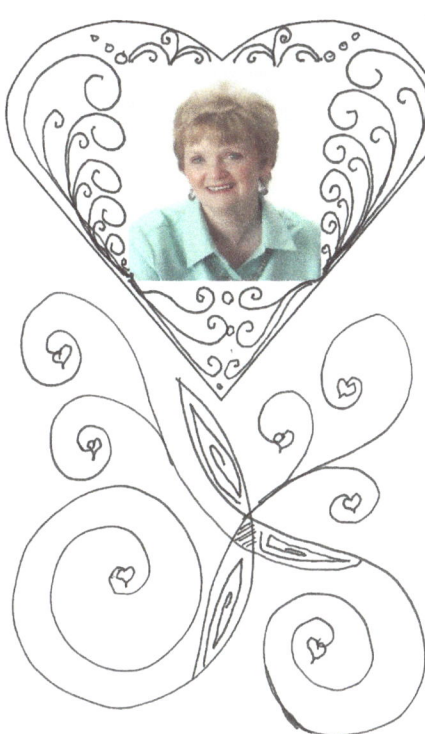

I0503049

My name is Jeanne Paglio , and I'm a Certified Zentangle Instructor. (CZT)

This book is intended for you to practice the art of tangling by filling in the empty tiles offered within these pages.

Other tiles are for your enjoyment. They are not meant to be taken and taught from.

This book was inspired by Rick Roberts and Maria Thomas, whose works are inspirational. I thank them for all they have shared and what they continue to share.

Zentangle is a registered trademark of Rick Roberts & Maria Thomas.

For additional information on Zentangle and Rick and Maria, refer to:

www.zentangle.com

Tools of the trade....
Pen .01 Micron—black
Pencil - for shading
Blending stump - for smudging

Sakura Pens (a variety)

Markers - for coloring
(Staedtler or Copic markers for example)

Watercolor pencils - Derwent

Websites to view.....
www.decorativeartistry.us
www.zentangle.com

Blogs to read....
http://zenoftangling.blogspot.com

Sakura Glaze Pens

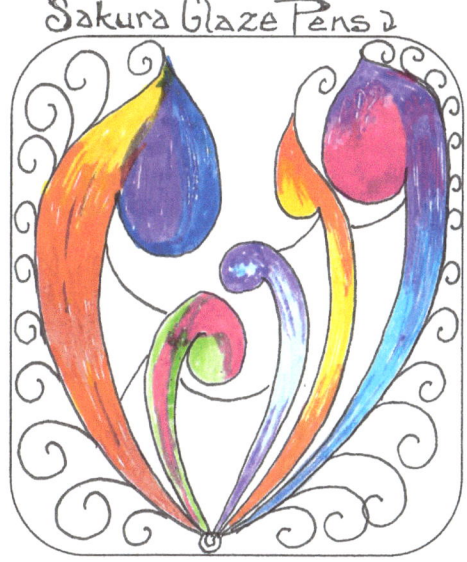

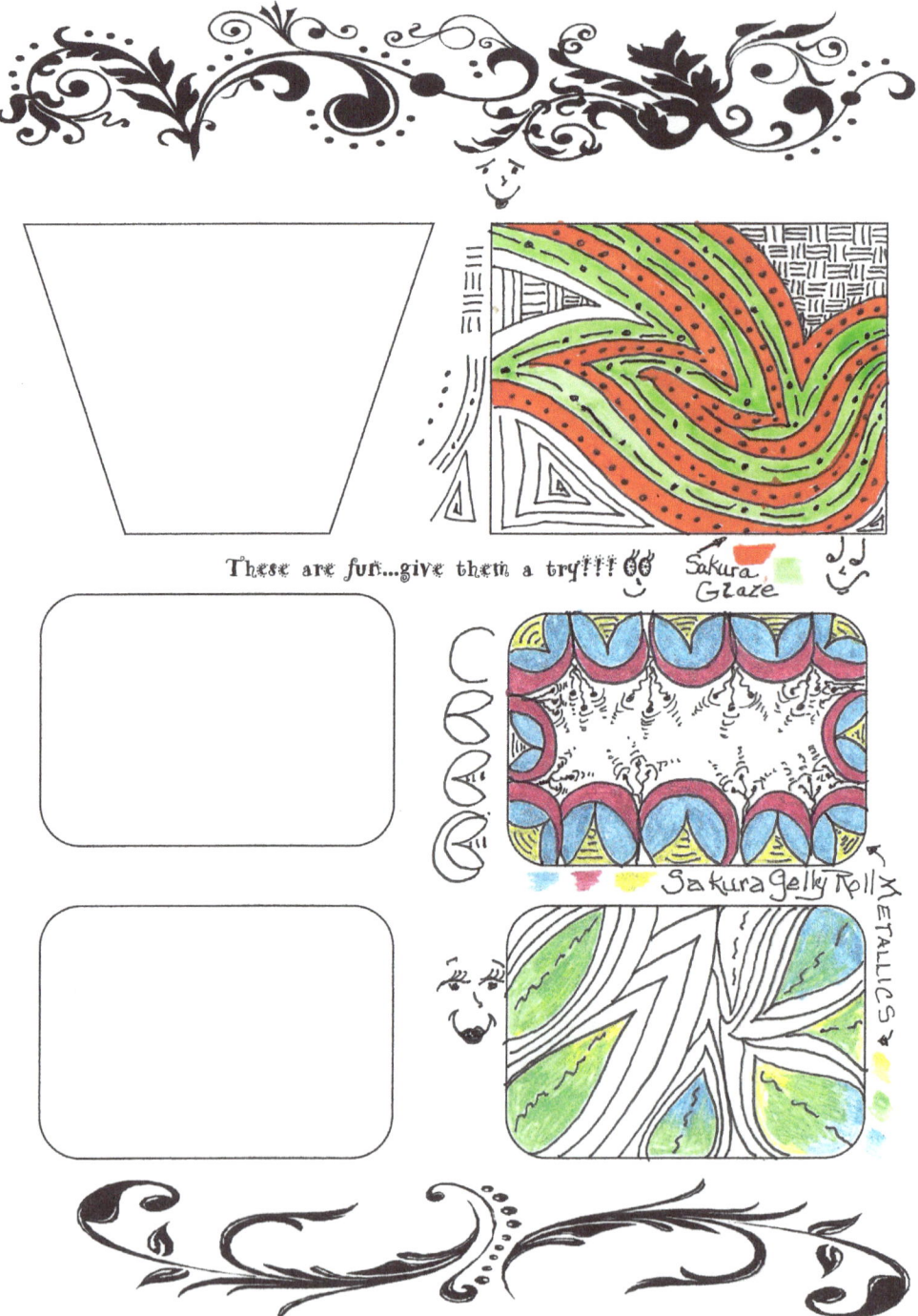

These are fun...give them a try!!! 😊😊   Sakura Glaze

Sakura Gelly Roll METALLICS

To add depth to your design, don't forget to shade with a pencil and smooch using a blending stump or your finger tip.

Build your tangle using a string. A tangle without a string can also be interesting. Try your hand at it and see for yourself how the design changes when using free space.

Breathe....Relax.....Enjoy.....

Sakura Souffle Pens

Now....add color to the mix. You can use markers or play with watercolor pencils and move the color with a damp paint brush. Once your tangle is done using a black pen, add shading with the marker or pencil for effect. Color will change the look.

There are no mistakes... only opportunities.....

Tangle away...

3

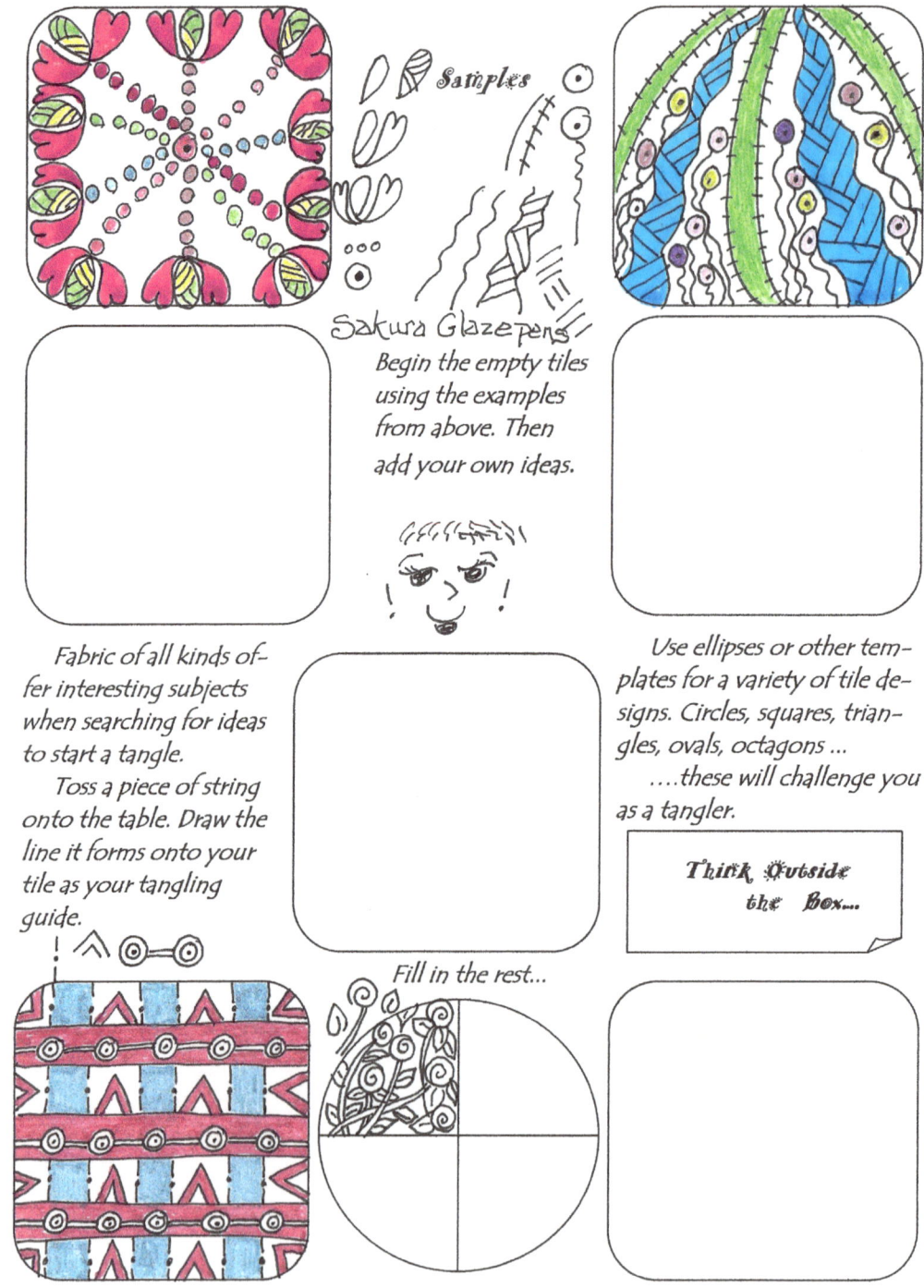

Samples

Sakura Glaze pens

Begin the empty tiles using the examples from above. Then add your own ideas.

Fabric of all kinds offer interesting subjects when searching for ideas to start a tangle.

Toss a piece of string onto the table. Draw the line it forms onto your tile as your tangling guide.

Use ellipses or other templates for a variety of tile designs. Circles, squares, triangles, ovals, octagons ...

....these will challenge you as a tangler.

Think Outside the Box....

Fill in the rest...

4

Symbols are *fun* to tangle. They can be large or small, fat or thin, capitalized or lower case...Just imagine how enjoyable it would be to make a greeting card using tangled letters or numbers.

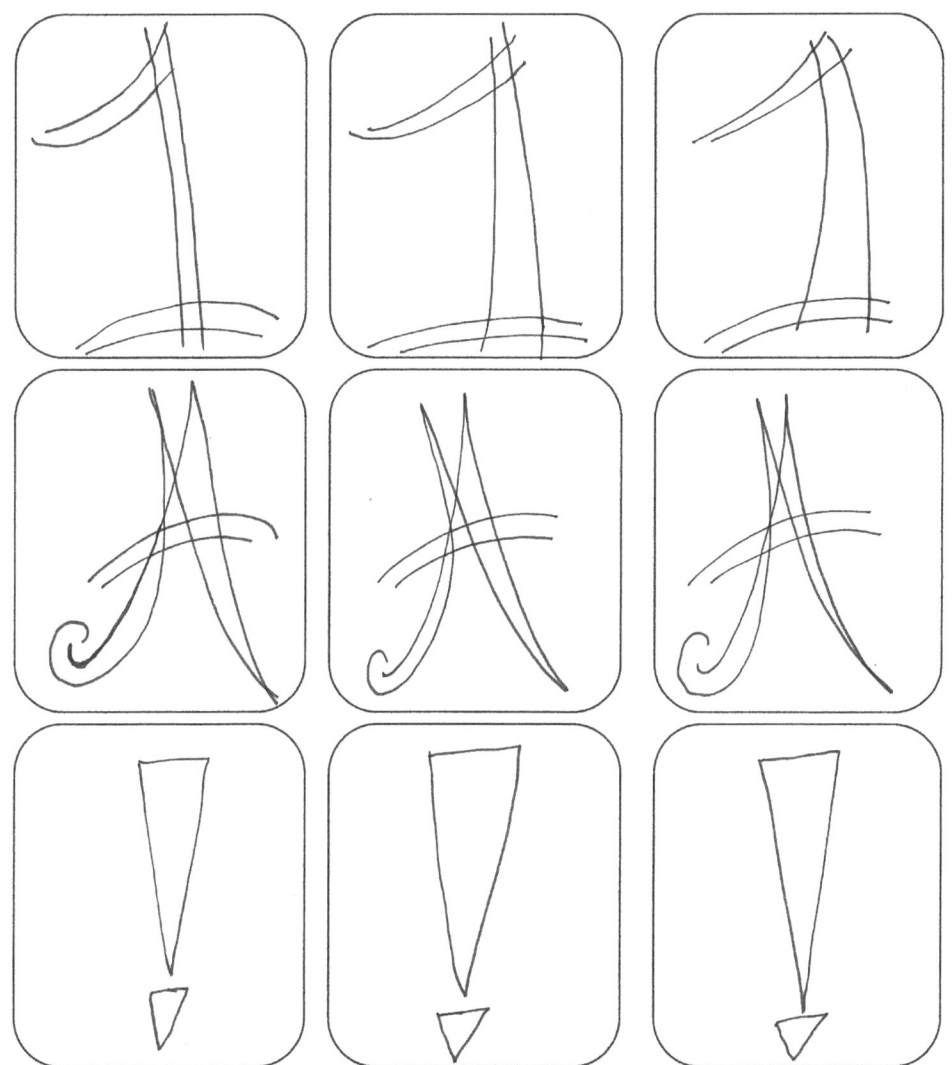

Let your imagination run wild. Add swirls, leaves, balls, bulbs, sparkles, twigs, buds, frogs, toads, petals, whatever you can think of. They don't have to be perfect since there are   No Mistakes....Only Opportunities.

Tangle to renew your mind and spirit!!!!

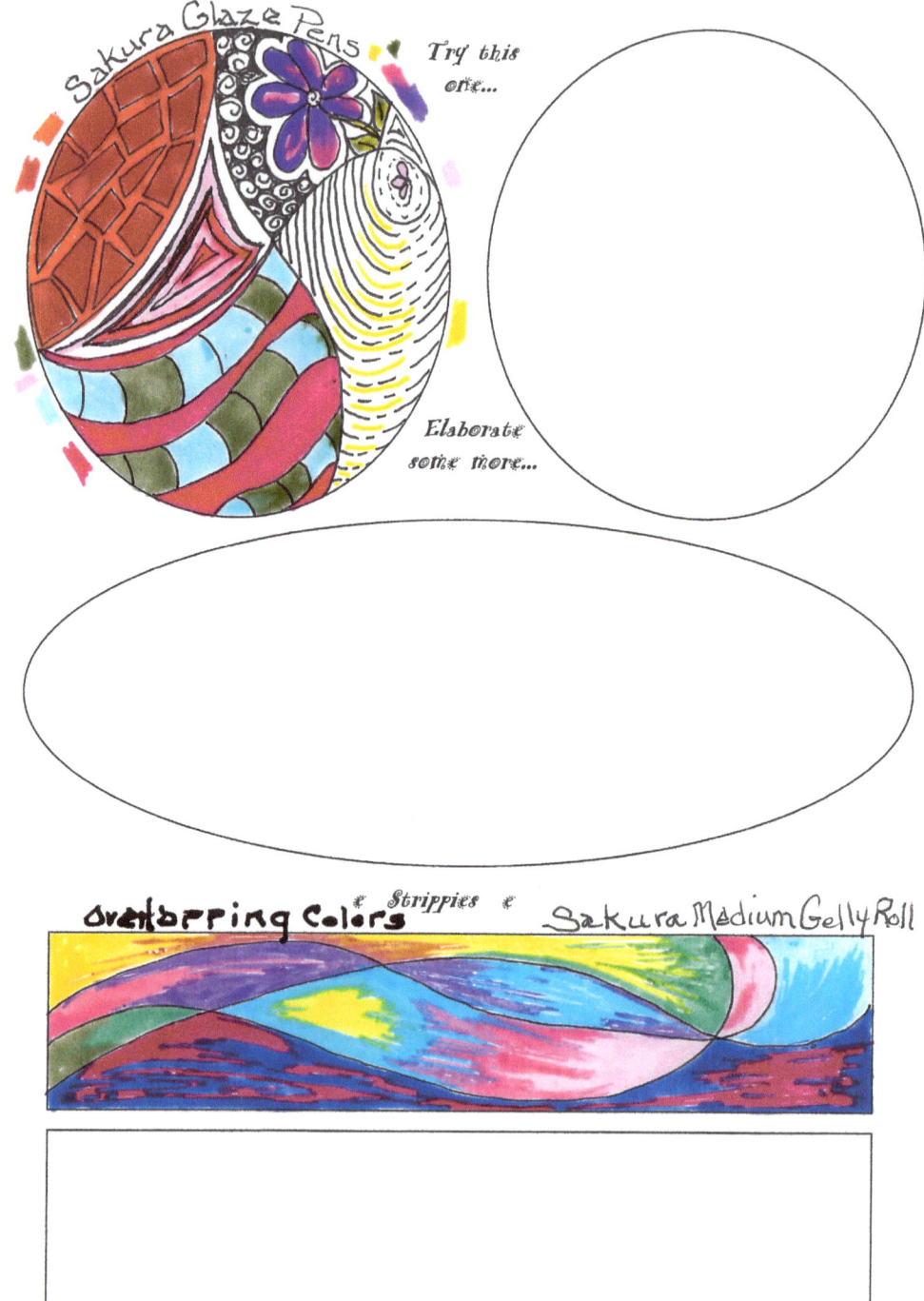

Sakura Glaze Pens

Try this one...

Elaborate some more...

Overlapping Colors & Strippies & Sakura Medium Gelly Roll

Have fun with color...

Fill in the shapes below

Pencil Shaded

Sakura gelly Roll Metallic

Blender Smooshed

Color a little or Color a lot

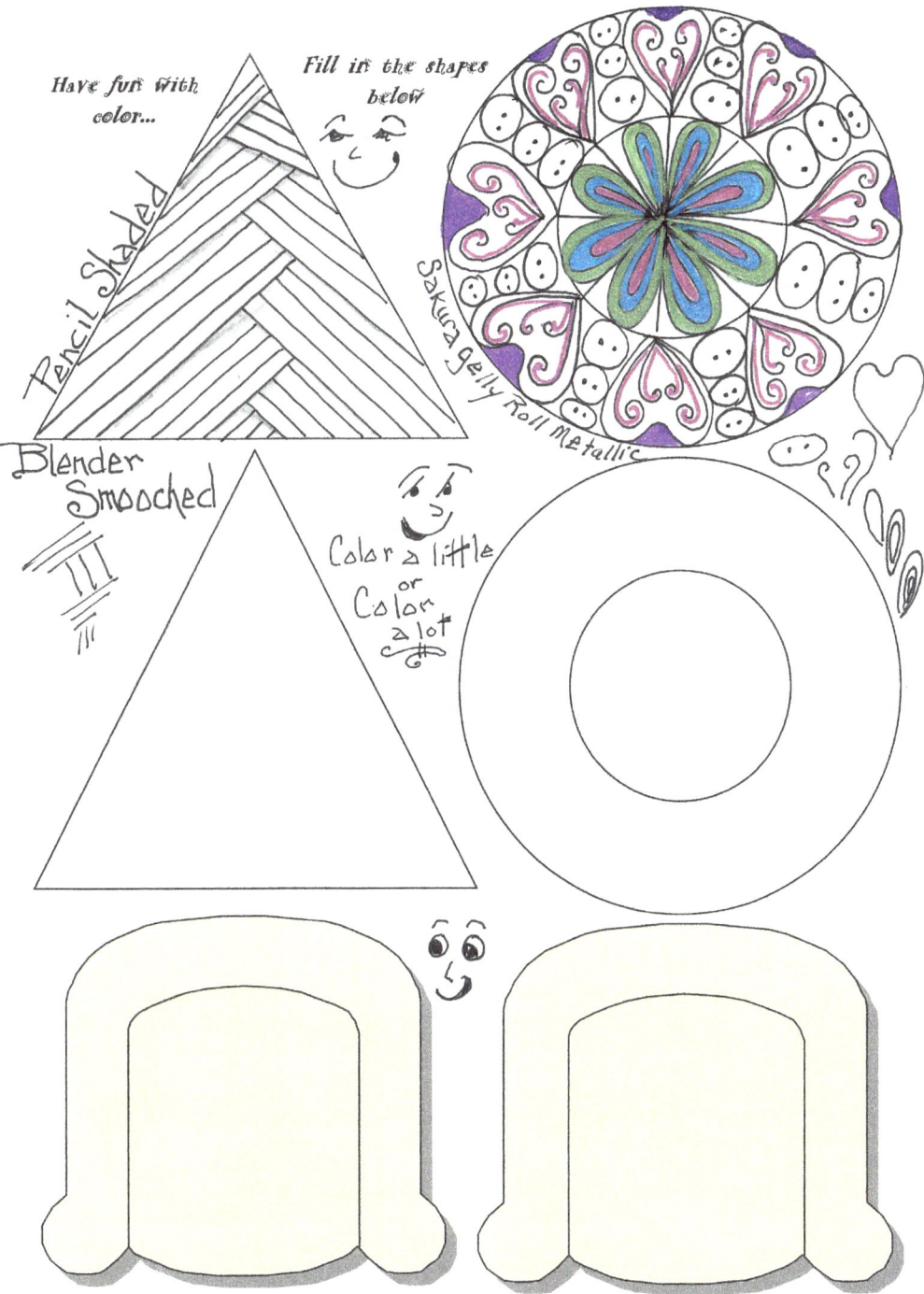

Glue a photo onto the paper!!!!
Embellish around the picture.

Relax

Breathe

Renew your

Spirit...

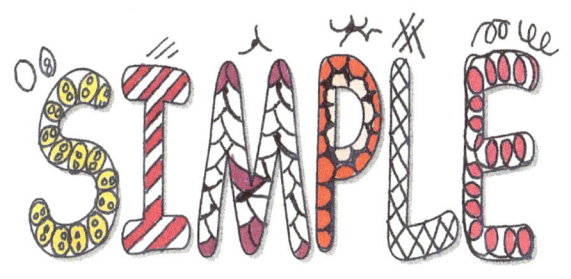

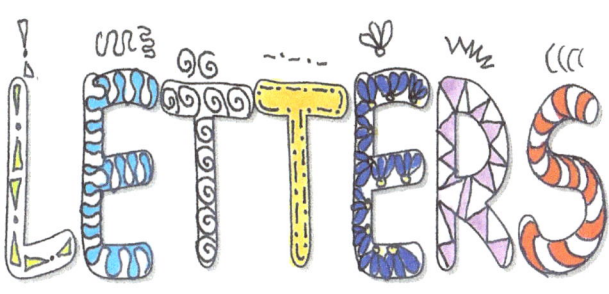

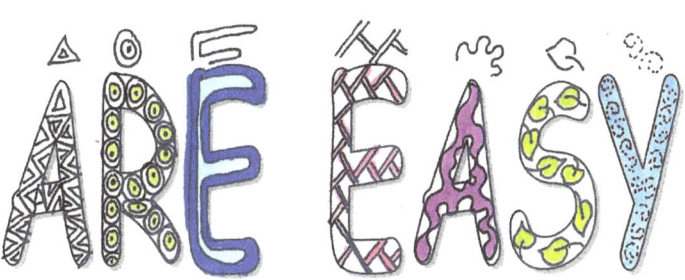

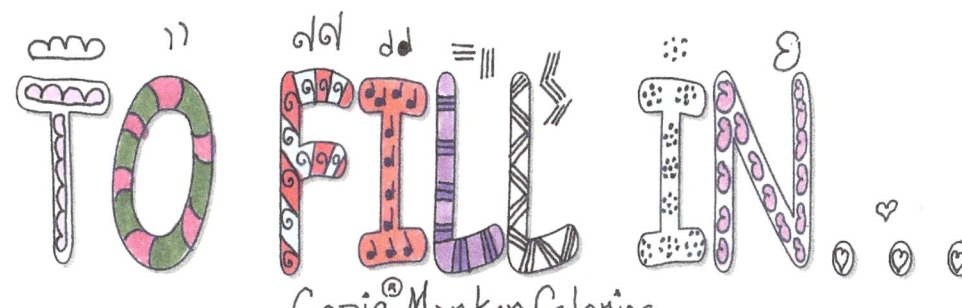

Copic® Marker Coloring
See how easy it is?

SIMPLE LETTERS ARE EASY TO FILL IN...

Go ahead, give it a try.
Embellish inside and out....

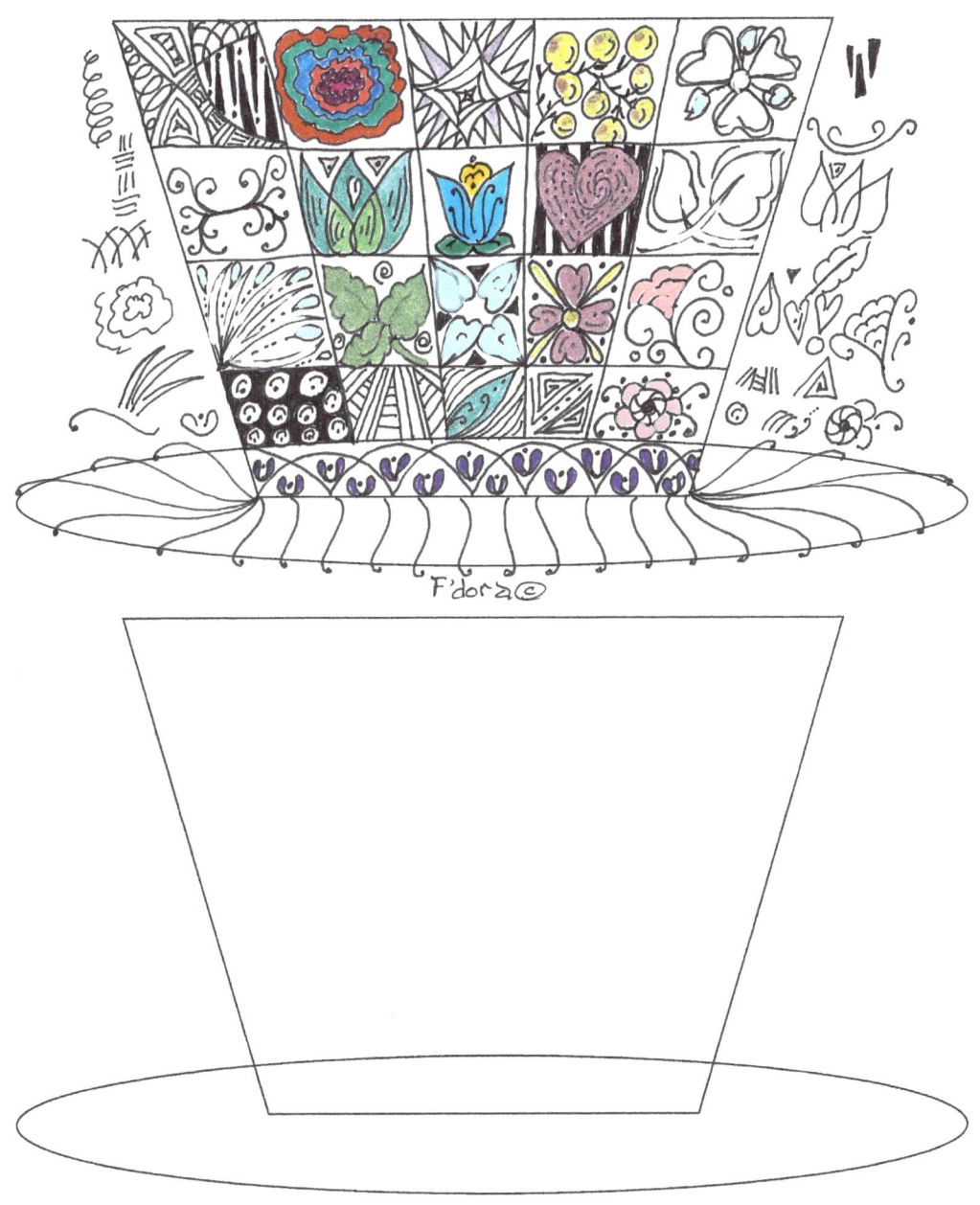

F'dora©

Try this hat on for size. Fill in the second one using the designs
offered or your own. See what happens...

11

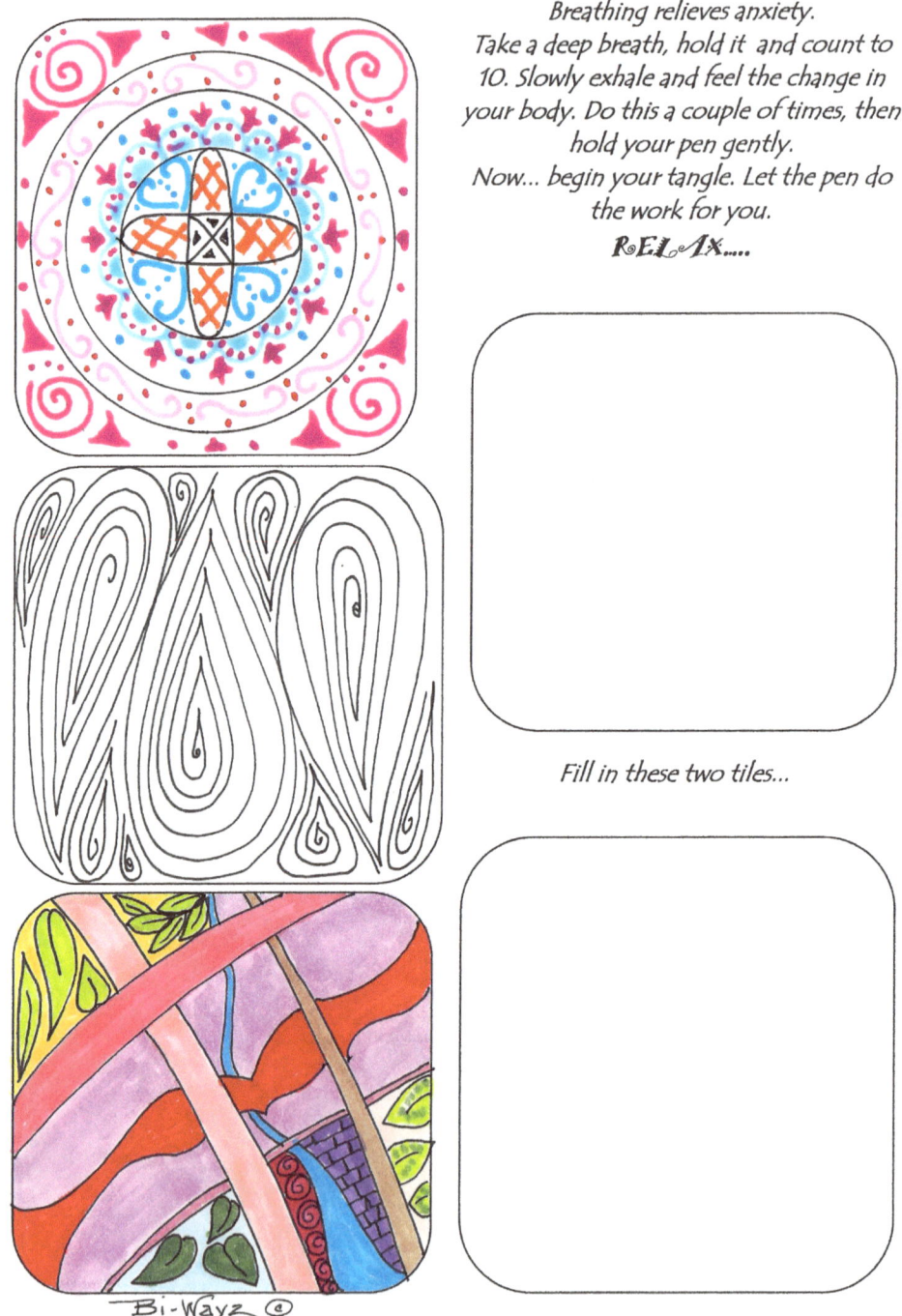

Breathing relieves anxiety.
Take a deep breath, hold it and count to
10. Slowly exhale and feel the change in
your body. Do this a couple of times, then
hold your pen gently.
Now... begin your tangle. Let the pen do
the work for you.
RELAX.....

Fill in these two tiles...

Bi-Wayz ©

12

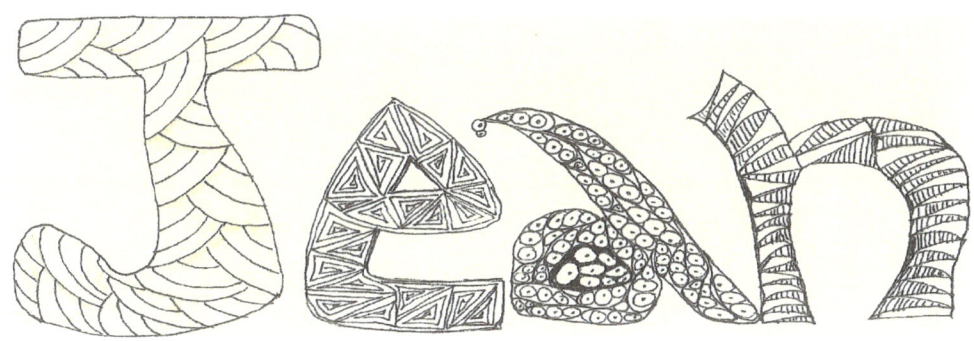

I rarely choose specific colors, I simply use what comes to hand first. To enhance marker colors, re-apply the same color again to add depth or shadow to the image!

ROPE ©

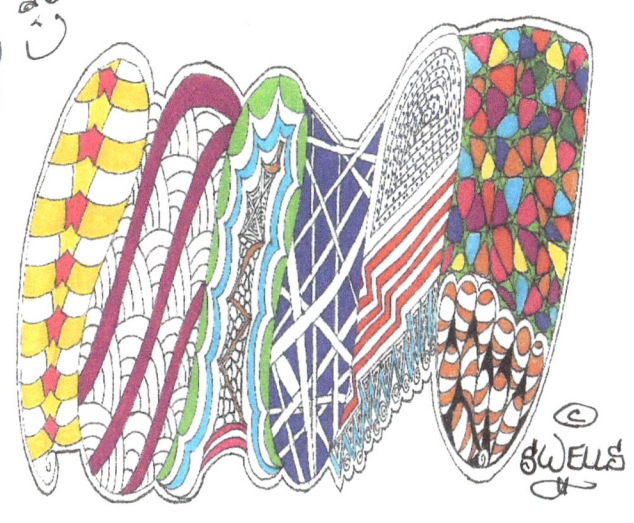

SWELLS ©

By filling in part of an image or all of it with color you let the white of the paper be your contrast. When working with a monochromatic palette, the white of the paper makes a perfect backdrop.

Try a variety of markers or colored pens to see what results work best for you. Markers are wonderful. There are many brands on the market that work well.

Sakura®Gelly Roll pens are a treat to work with.

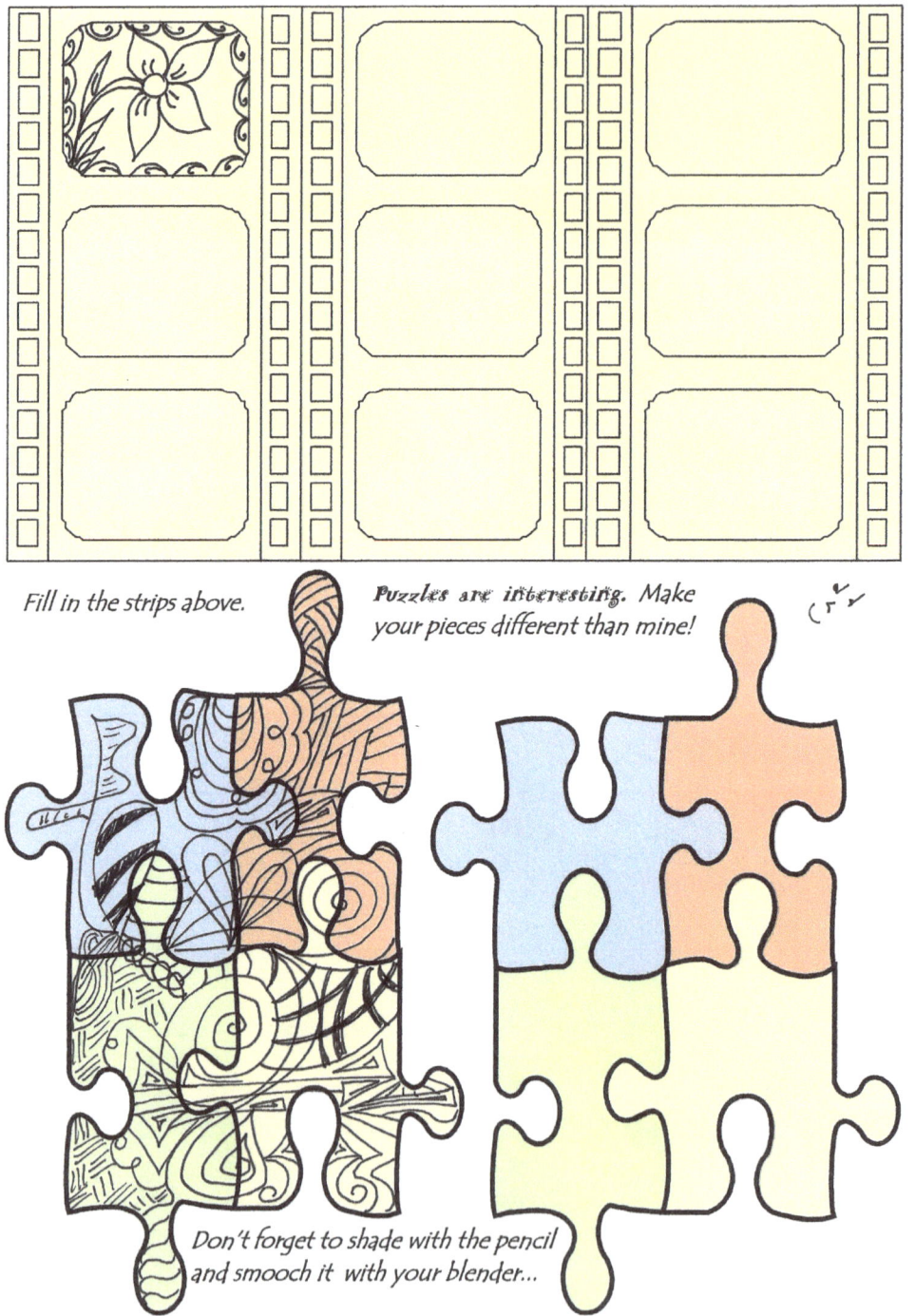

Fill in the strips above.

Puzzles are interesting. Make your pieces different than mine!

Don't forget to shade with the pencil and smooch it with your blender...

14

Picture This ...

Fill in the stars. Use color or just black and white. It's Your choice. Relax..... Enjoy!!!!

Sakura Glaze Pens used here!

Various shaped boxes and bubbles can lead to interesting creations.
Here are some for you to see and some to do.

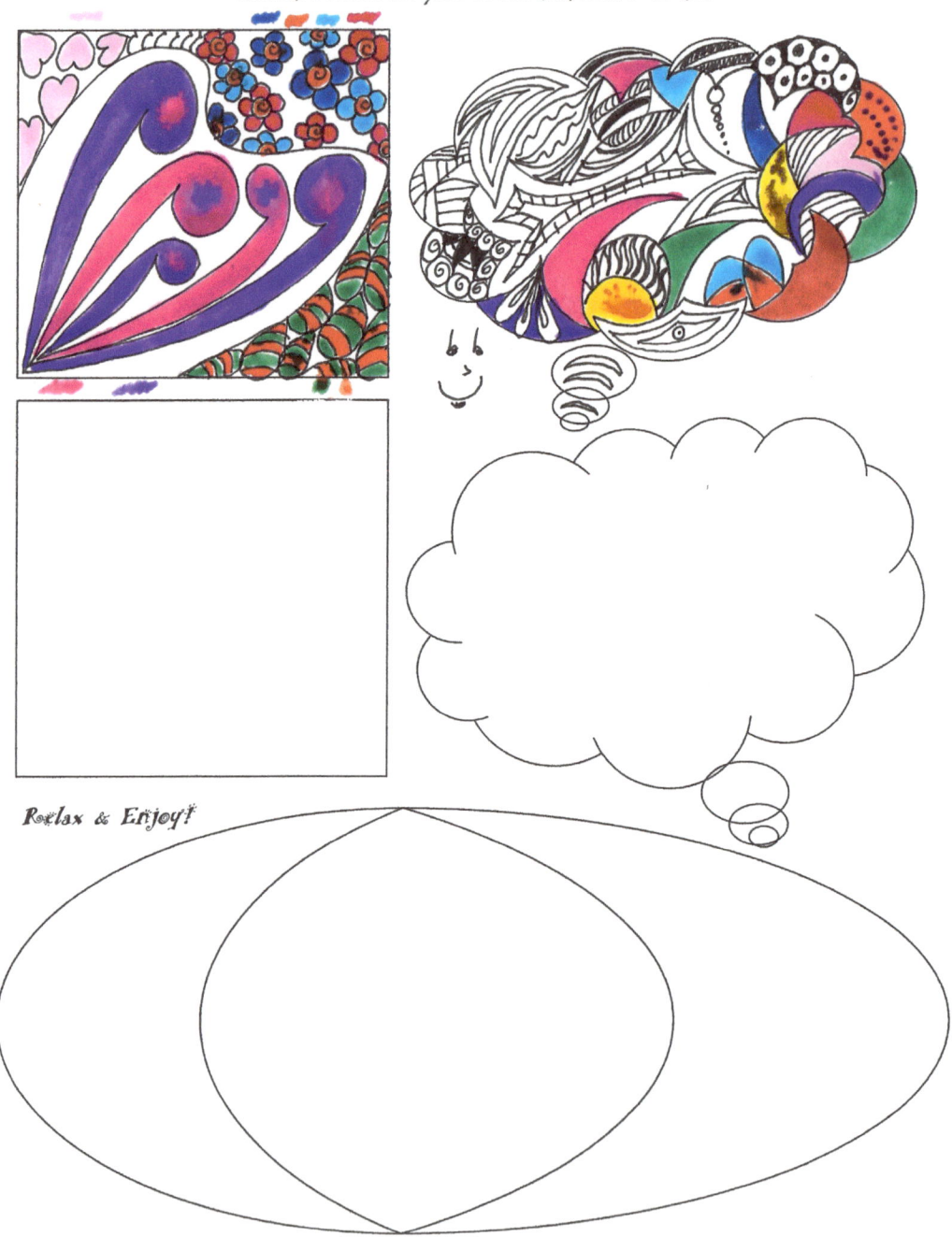

Relax & Enjoy!

All the frames are provided to help you think _outside_ the box... Enjoy coming up
with your own designs by adding a string to them.

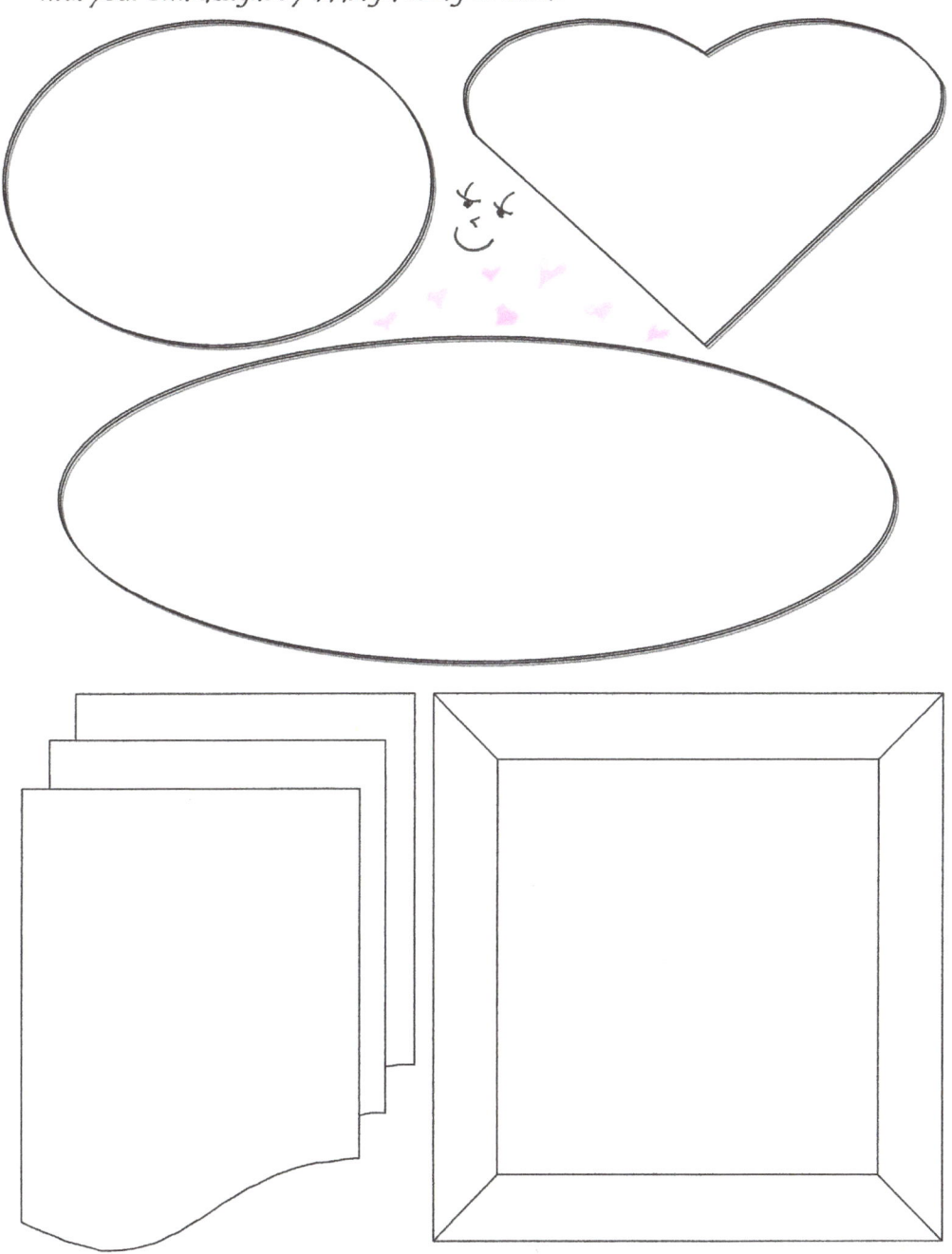

The tiles here are strung for you. See what you can do with them.

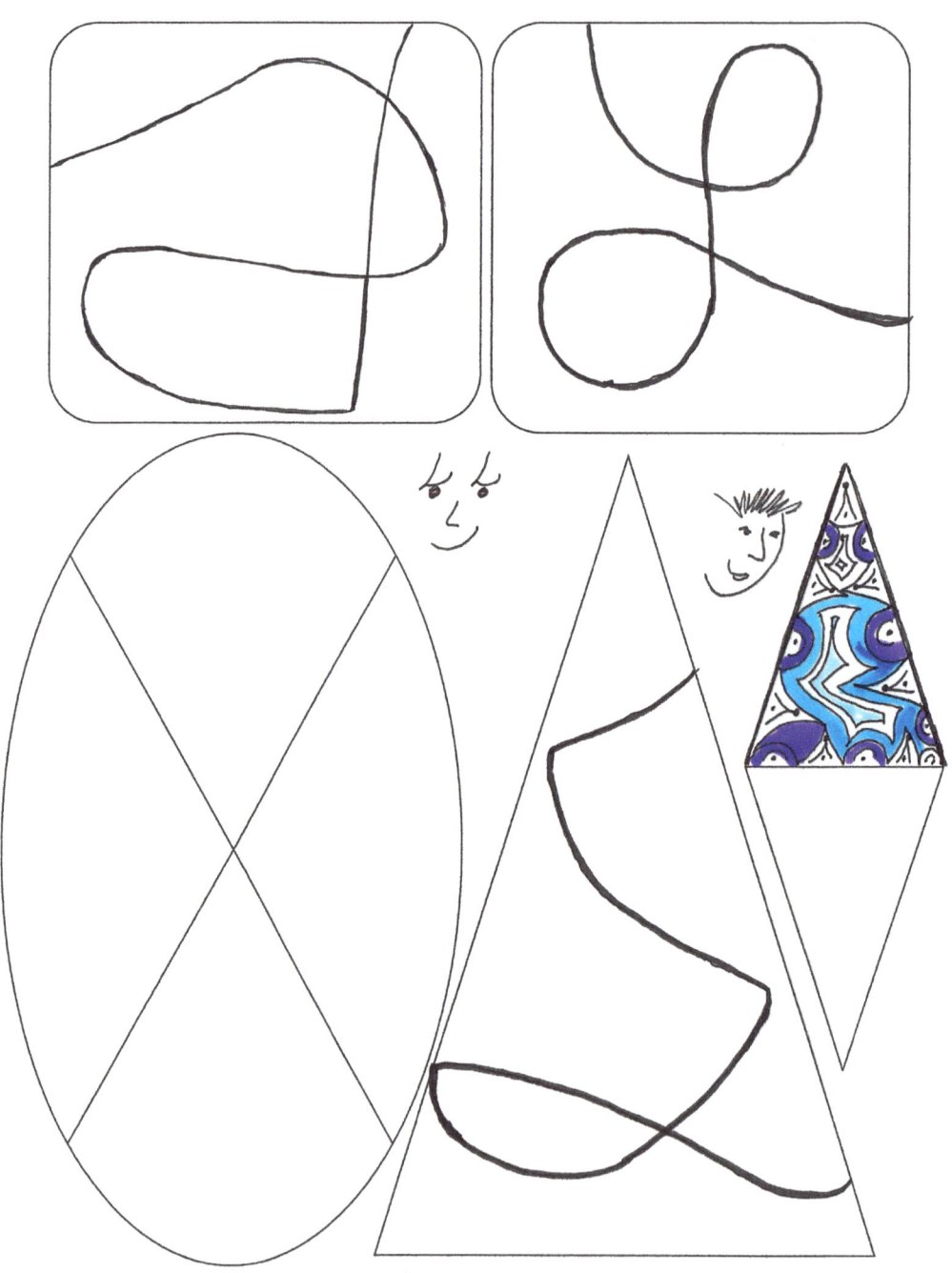

Tangle these shapes.

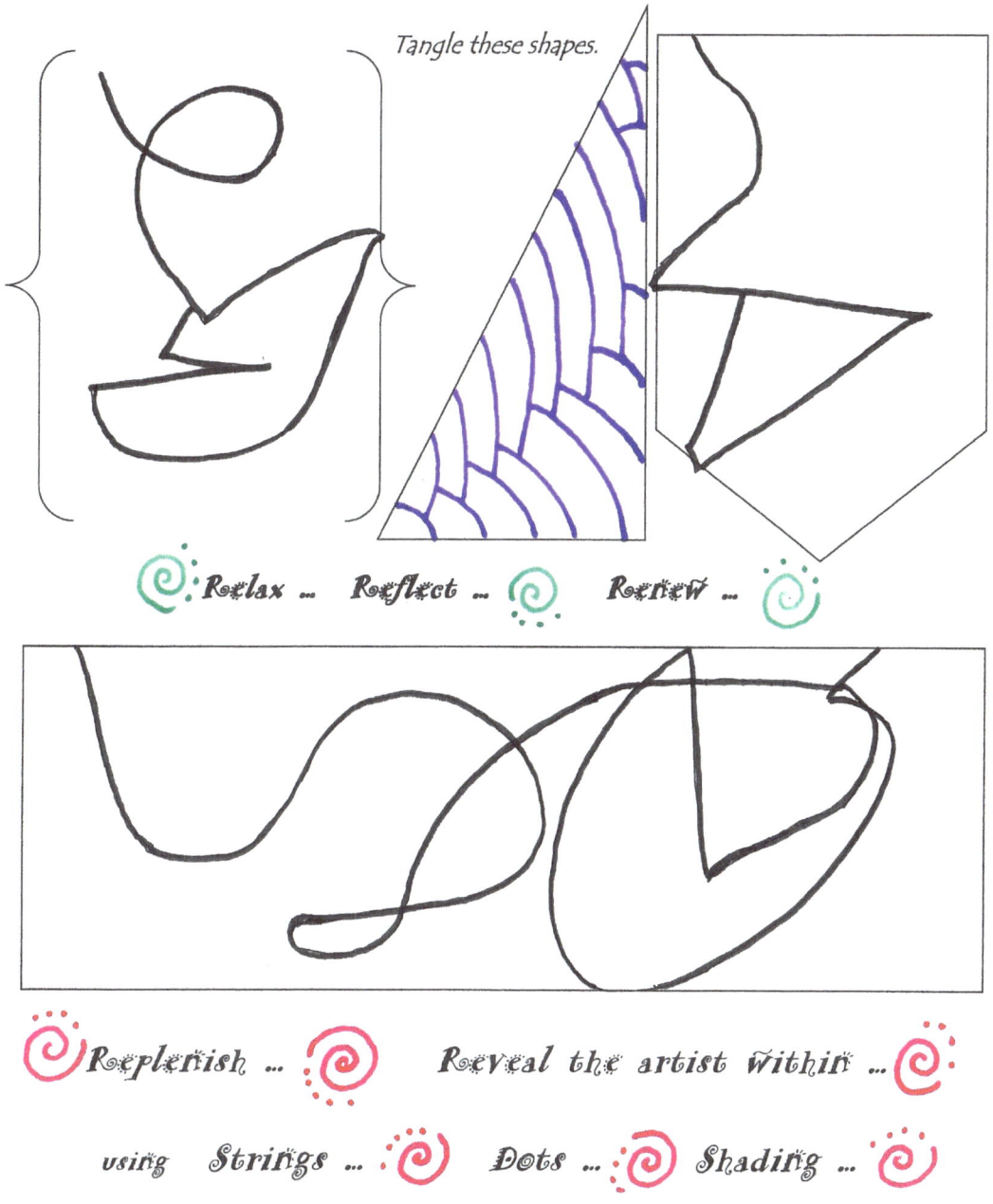

Relax ... Reflect ... Renew ...

Replenish ... Reveal the artist within ...

using Strings ... Dots ... Shading ...

Replenish your spirit by taking time to tangle everyday. Even if the time is brief, the benefits are great. As a confidence builder, an anger management tool or as a pleasure, tangling daily will help you relax.

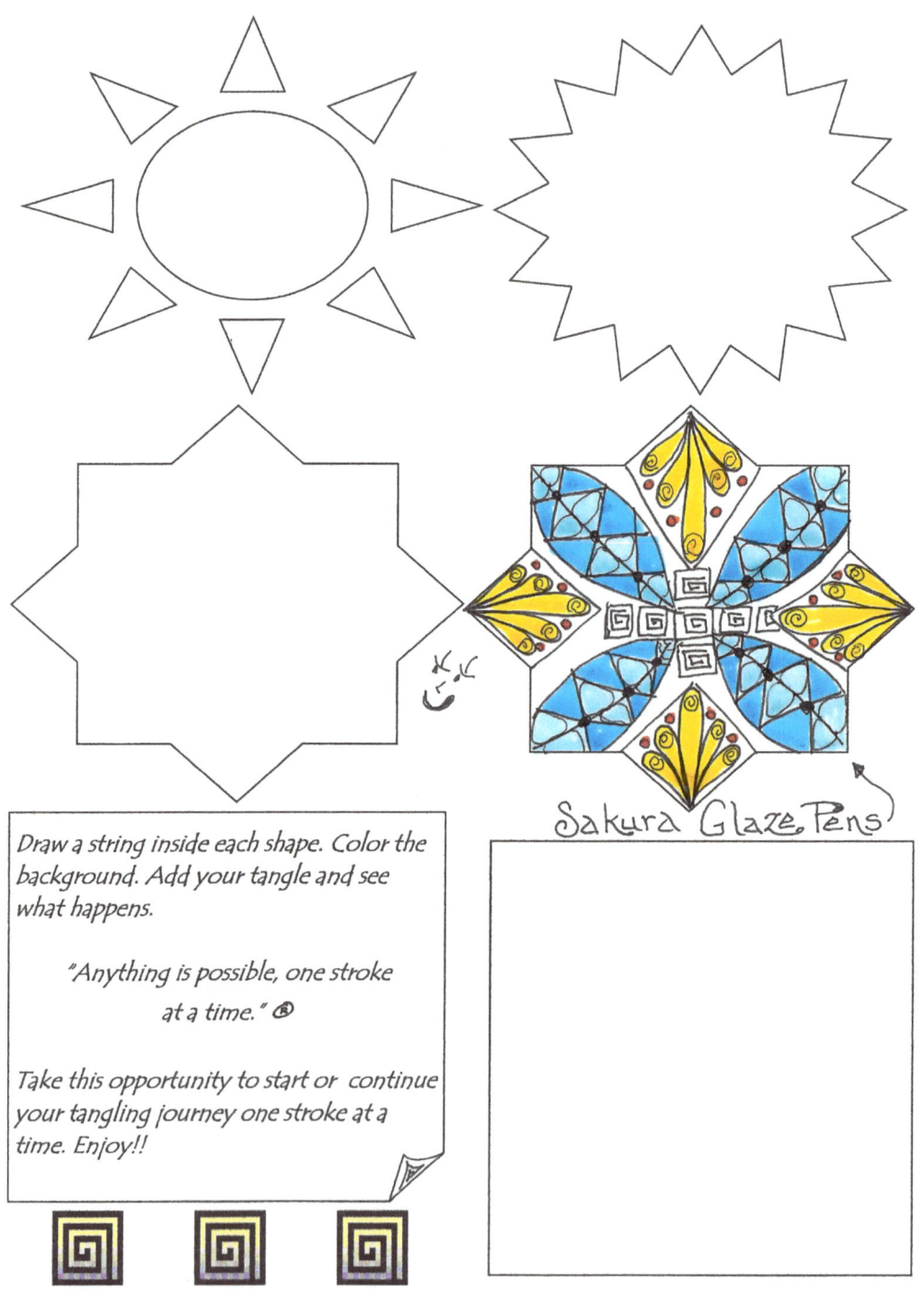

Draw a string inside each shape. Color the background. Add your tangle and see what happens.

"Anything is possible, one stroke at a time." ☺

Take this opportunity to start or continue your tangling journey one stroke at a time. Enjoy!!

Sakura Glaze Pens

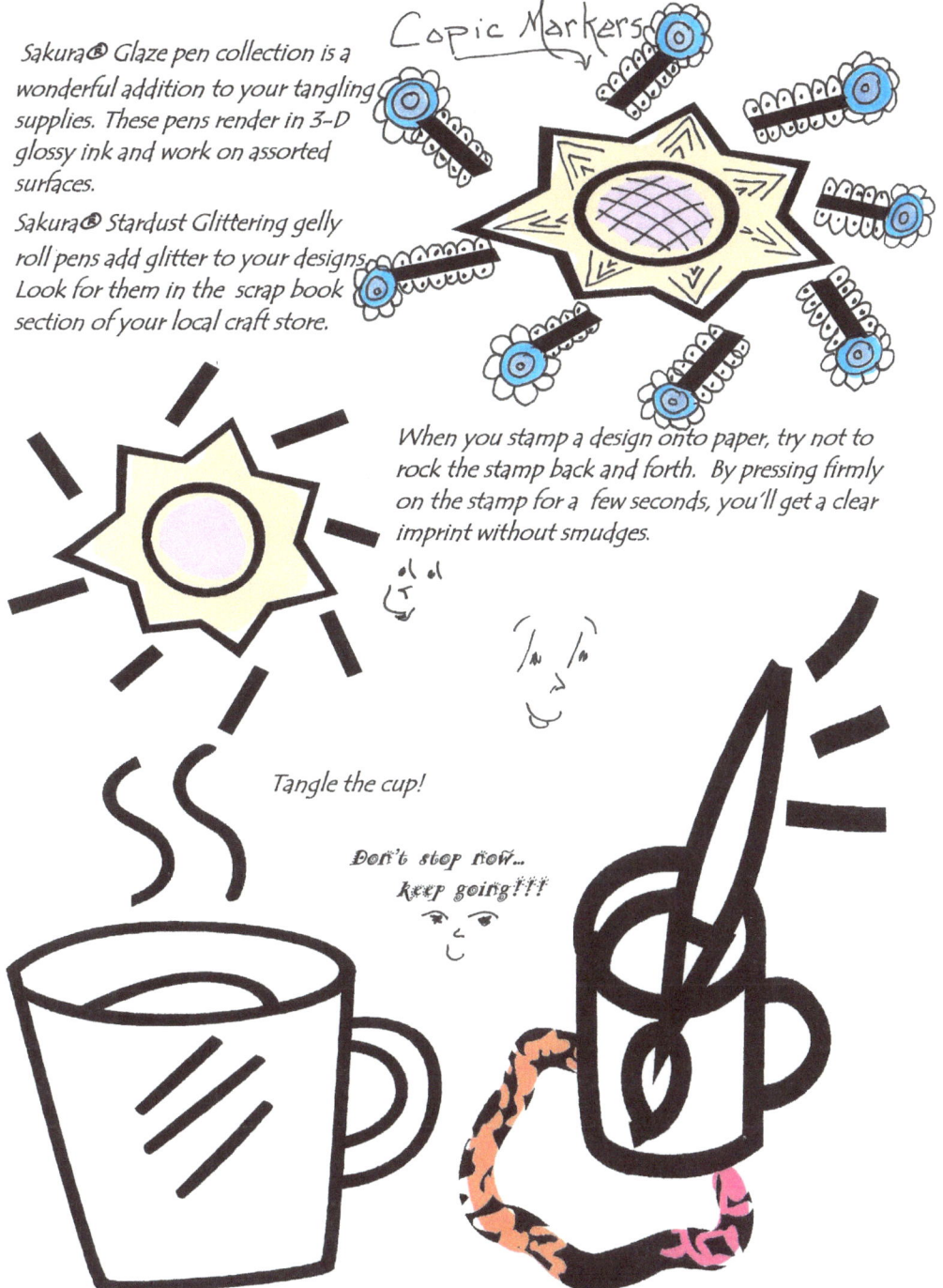

Sakura® Glaze pen collection is a wonderful addition to your tangling supplies. These pens render in 3-D glossy ink and work on assorted surfaces.

Sakura® Stardust Glittering gelly roll pens add glitter to your designs. Look for them in the scrap book section of your local craft store.

Copic Markers

When you stamp a design onto paper, try not to rock the stamp back and forth. By pressing firmly on the stamp for a few seconds, you'll get a clear imprint without smudges.

Tangle the cup!

Don't stop now... keep going!!!

21

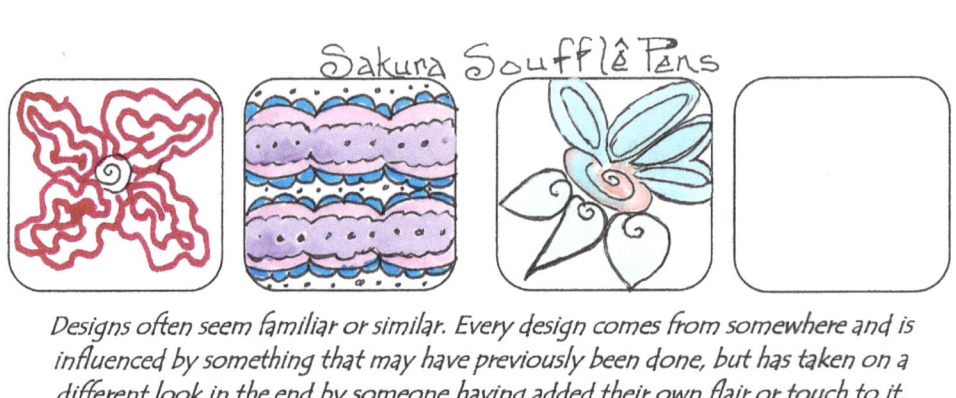

Sakura Soufflê Pens

Designs often seem familiar or similar. Every design comes from somewhere and is influenced by something that may have previously been done, but has taken on a different look in the end by someone having added their own flair or touch to it. Being inspired by another's work is okay.

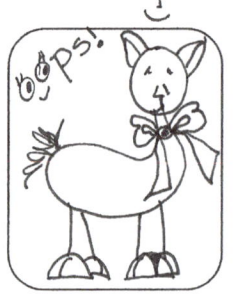

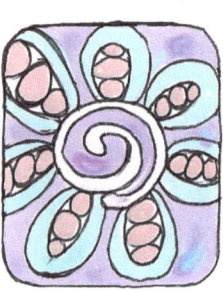

Work out your designs by allowing your body and mind to relax. If you pressure yourself, tangle lines are less likely to flow the way you hope they will.

Take a rest from your worries by tangling....

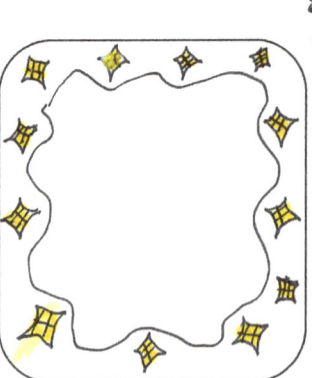

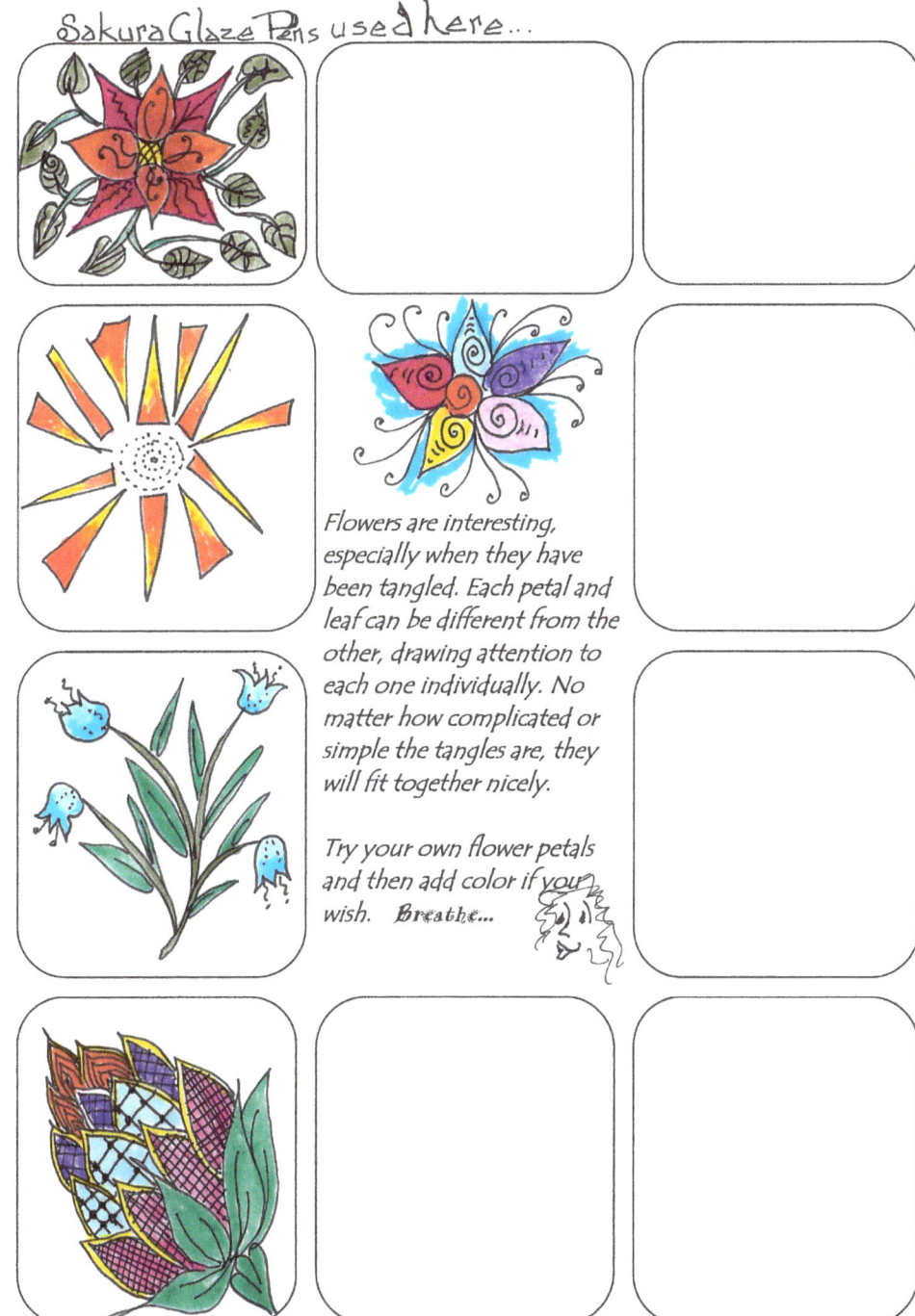

Flowers are interesting, especially when they have been tangled. Each petal and leaf can be different from the other, drawing attention to each one individually. No matter how complicated or simple the tangles are, they will fit together nicely.

Try your own flower petals and then add color if you wish. *Breathe...*

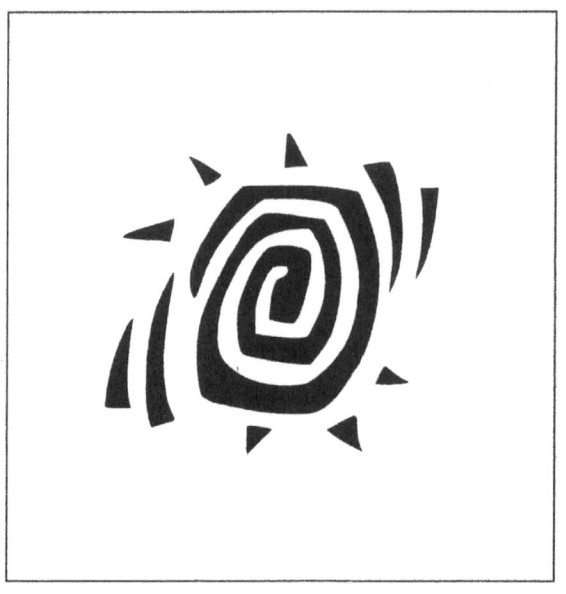

Embellish these two designs.
Finish with color .
You'll be surprised at the results.
Insert a box below and create your
own tangle.

Keep going. Use some of the ideas
from other pages to inspire you.

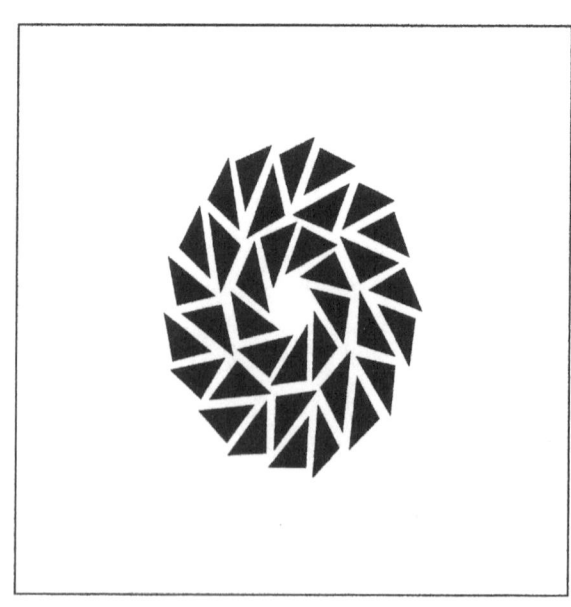

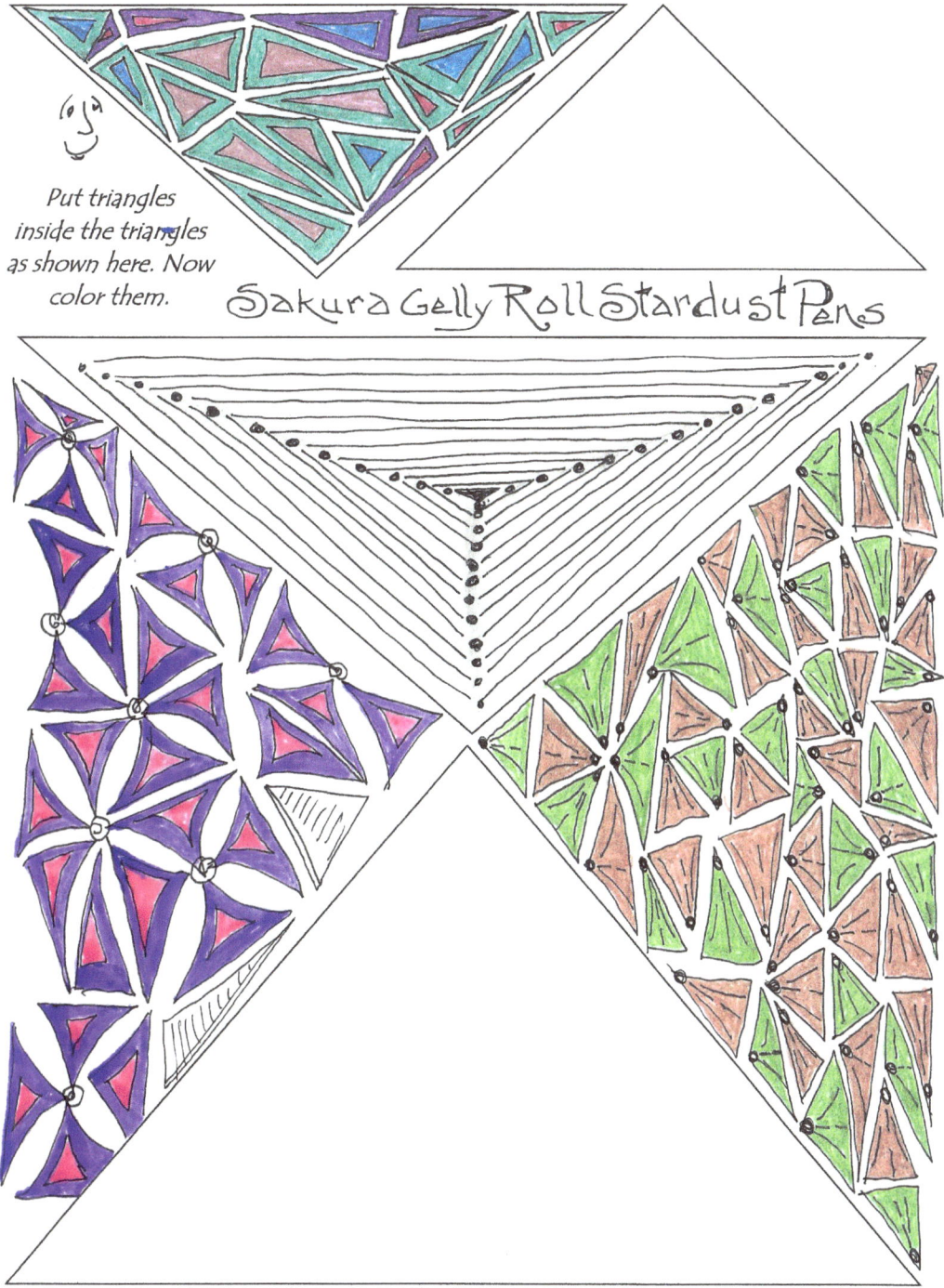

Put triangles inside the triangles as shown here. Now color them.

Sakura Gelly Roll Stardust Pens

Rubber stamp your way to happiness. Gently rub the rubber face of the stamp with the ink pad. No need to press hard on the pad. Now....firmly press the inked stamp straight onto a piece of scrap paper and lift the stamp. Refrain from rocking it back and forth, otherwise the lines might smudge. Once you have succeeded in achieving a nice stamped design, try it in the boxes above, add embellishments and color. Apply some stamped designs in the space below without a box, then embellish around them in a *free spirit* sort of way....

*Freestyle your tangles below. Instead of using boxes with dots in the corners, begin by drawing a string. Now take it from there by inserting your own tangles. **Enjoy the challenge.** Don't be concerned over having to draw a box with your pencil, simply let your imagination run wild.* ෨

Example

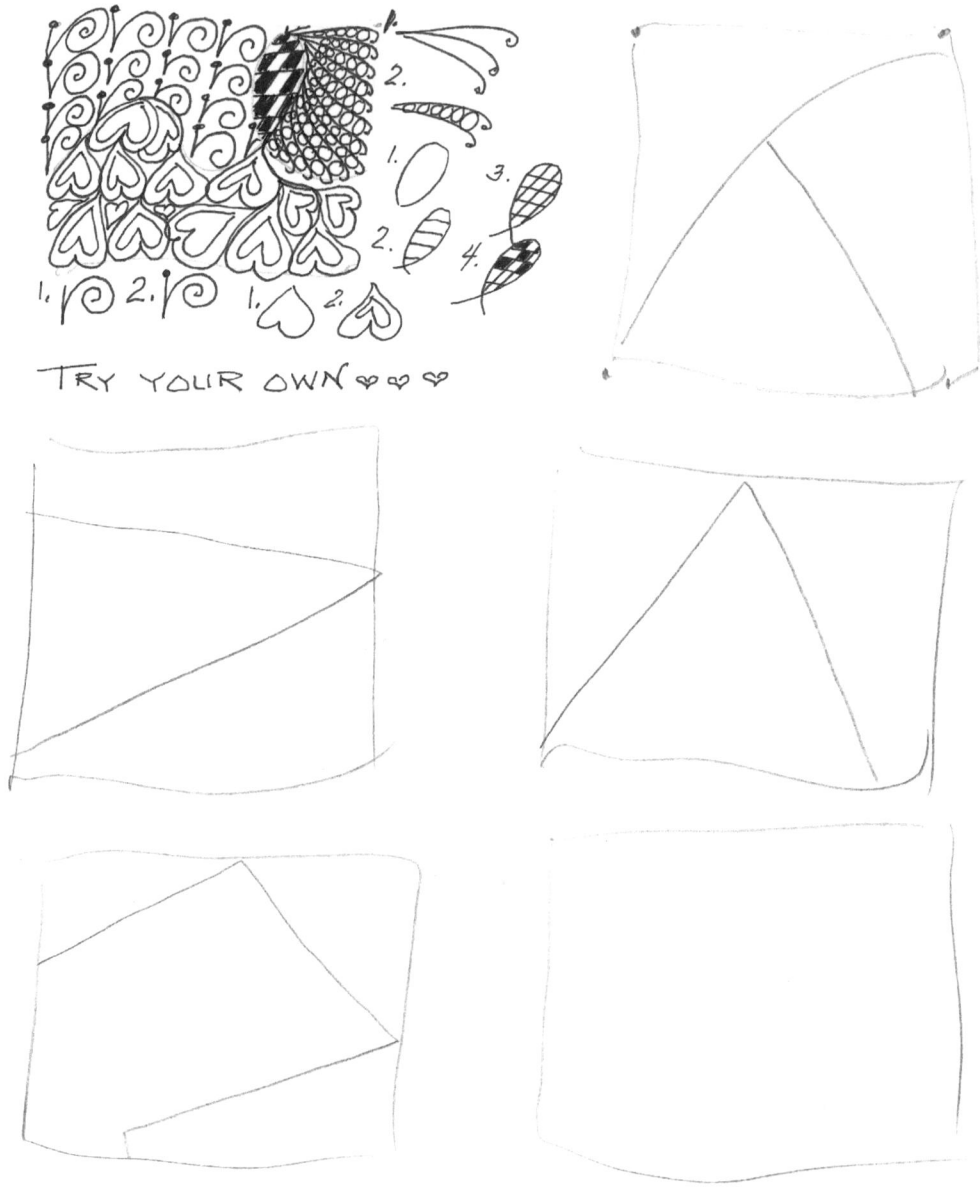

TRY YOUR OWN ♥♥♥

Allow the energy to flow into your body as you relax and breathe. As you become more and more involved in your tangle, you will notice how replenished you are. That is your "aha" moment! Enjoy yourself!!

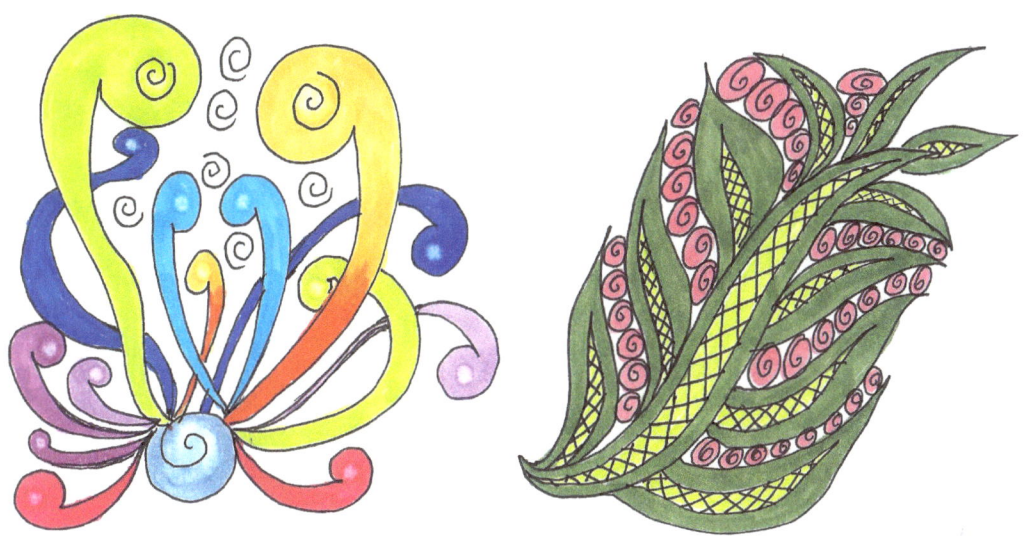

Colored with Copic Markers.

Make time to tangle every day. Even if it is for a brief period. Eventually you'll notice a change for the better as you de-stress your life. This is a great activity to share with family or friends. The benefits are wonderful.... Put yours below?...

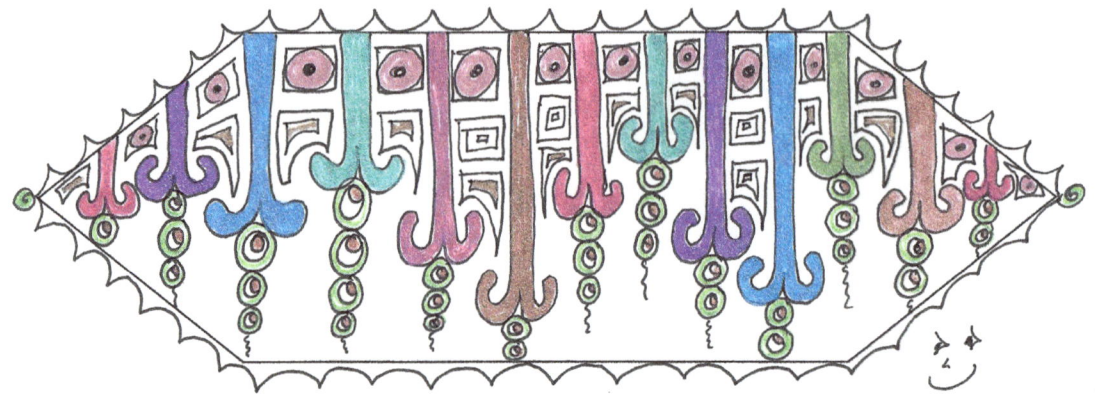

Stand up...stretch your arms above your head and reach for the sky. Breathe deeply, now bend over at the waist and shake your arms out as they hang toward the floor. Doesn't that feel good? Now repeat that 2-3 times. Then start tangling...

There truly is no wrong way to tangle. The best way to begin, when you are first learning this unique art form, is to use your pencil to place a dot in each corner of your tile. Connect the dots and draw a string in any shape you wish within the box. From there, you can start to tangle using your pen. Make any shapes, designs or ideas that pop into your head. No experience is necessary to create a tangled tile.

☙ Remember to hold the pen gently, let your hand guide you. ☙

1.   2.   3. Have fun ♥

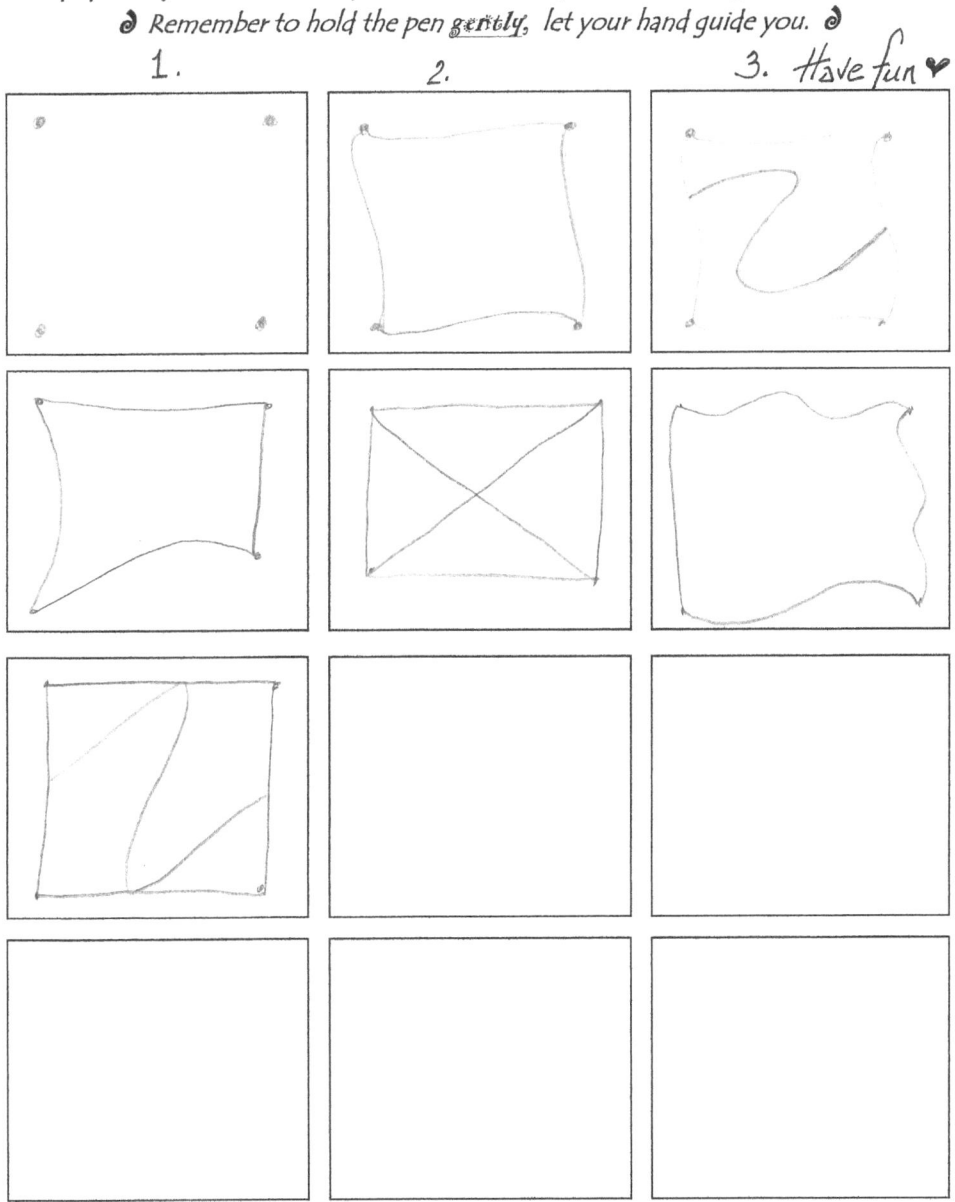

Staedtler Triplus Pens

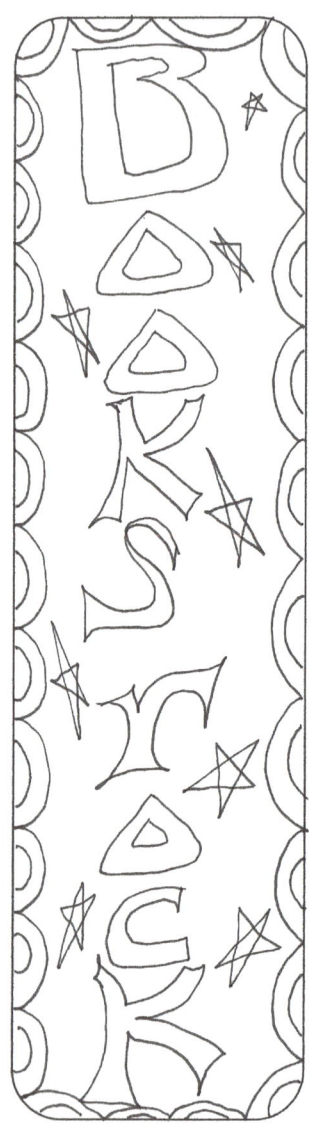

Put one here ↴

Book marks are easy to create. The busier the designs the more fun the tangles are . Try your hand at these. Then cut strips of card stock , watercolor paper or any paper you choose. Tangle them with a name or a design. They make perfect gifts when you need a small, but elegant gift for someone special.

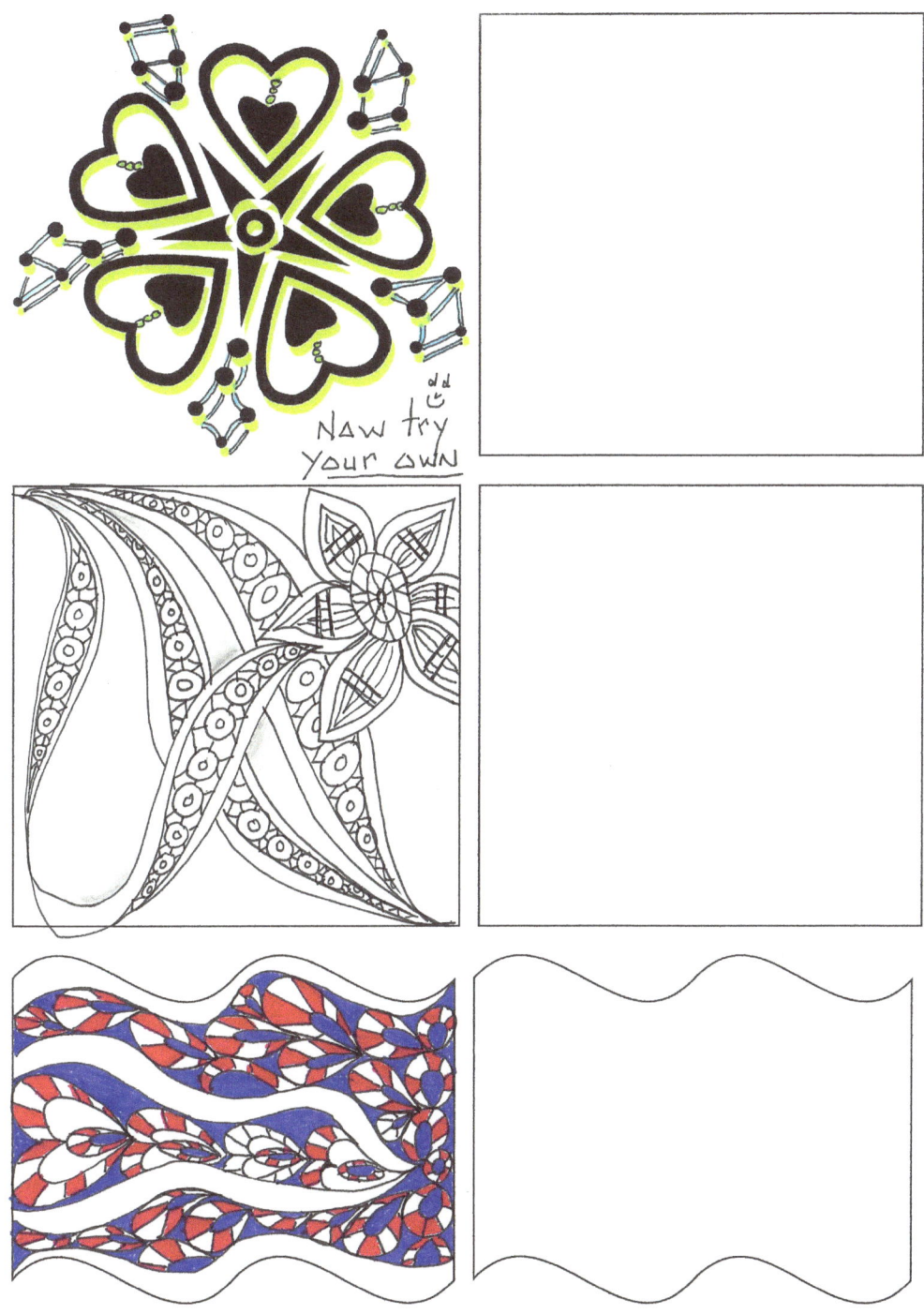

Now try
your own

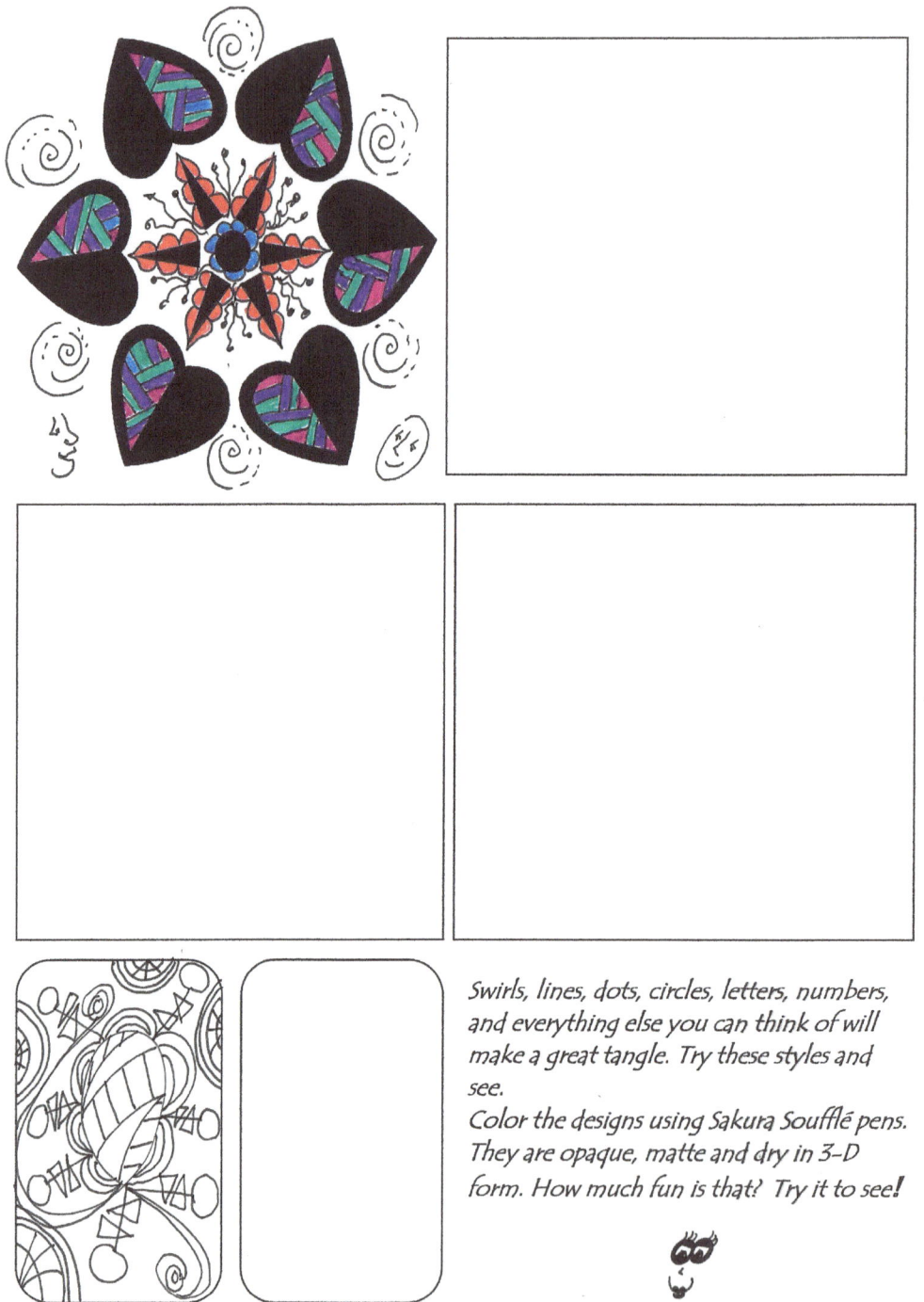

Swirls, lines, dots, circles, letters, numbers, and everything else you can think of will make a great tangle. Try these styles and see.

Color the designs using Sakura Soufflé pens. They are opaque, matte and dry in 3-D form. How much fun is that? Try it to see!

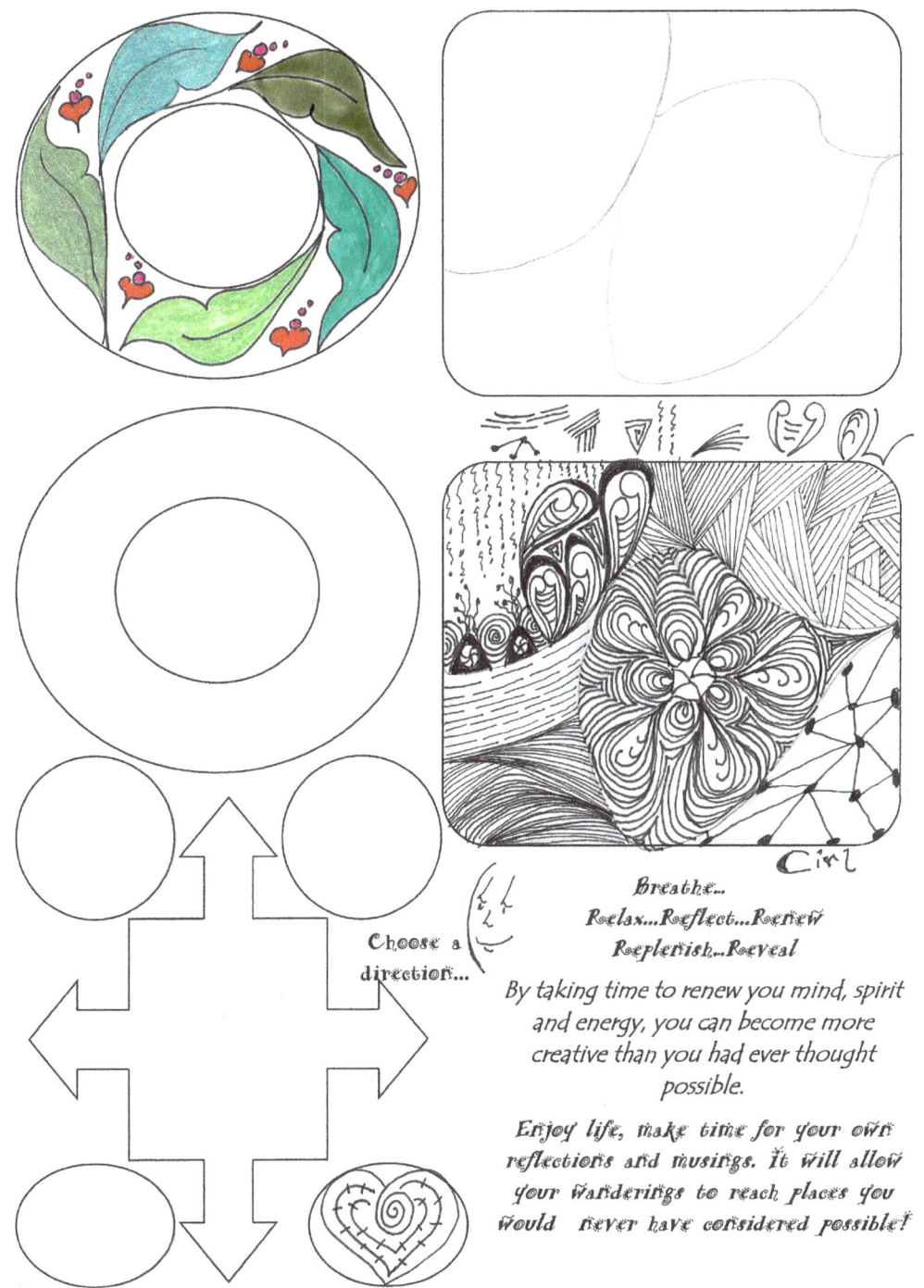

Cirl

Choose a direction...

Breathe...
Relax...Reflect...Renew
Replenish...Reveal

By taking time to renew you mind, spirit and energy, you can become more creative than you had ever thought possible.

Enjoy life, make time for your own reflections and musings. It will allow your wanderings to reach places you would never have considered possible!

Someone once said that sharing with others brings good things to you in return. It is so true. Find a bit of rainbow in each day, share it with someone you know or have recently met. It will enrich your life and theirs. Now tangle with them to improve both of your lives even more.

Sakura Gelly Roll Stardust Pens

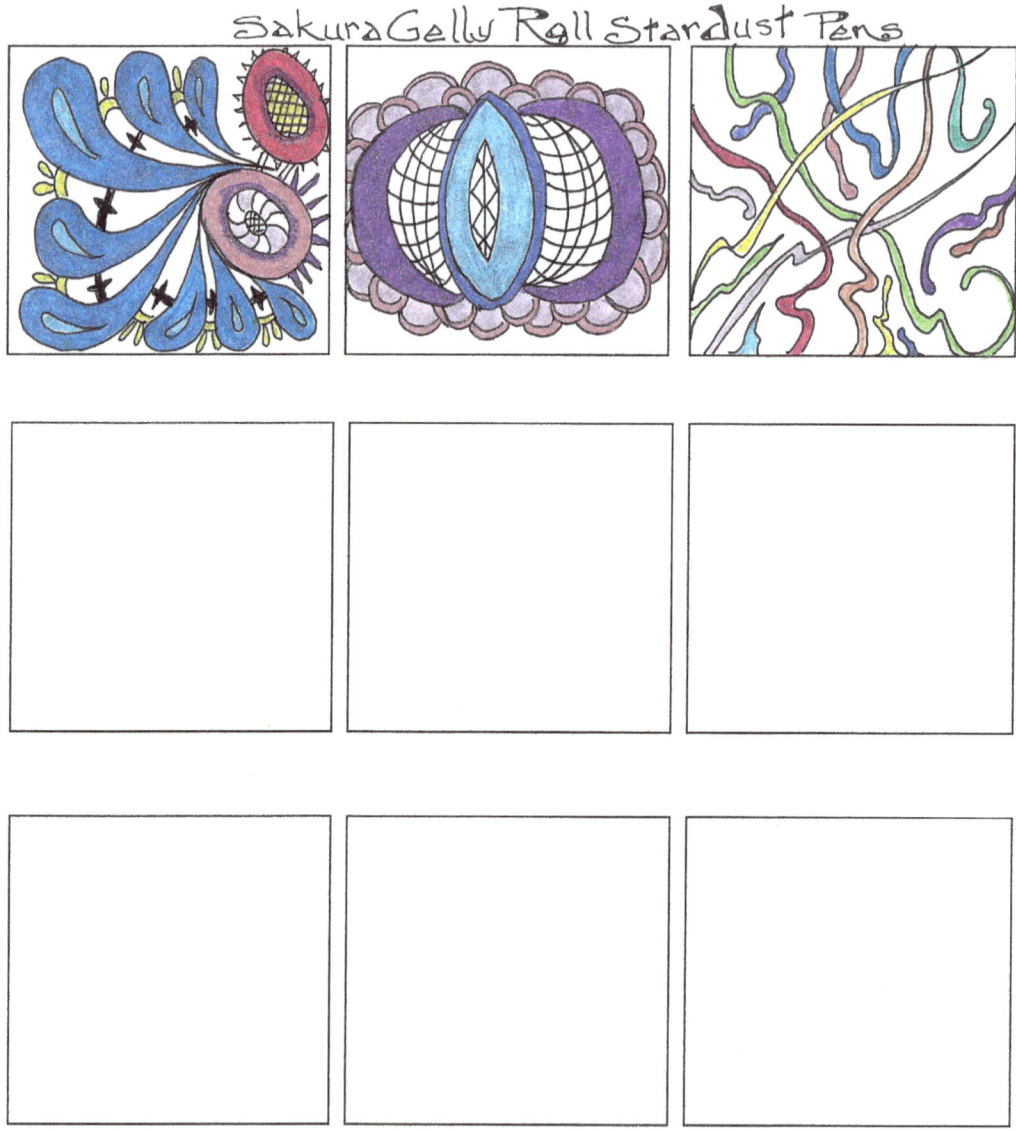

Tangling *fulfills* the need to create. It is what *you* want it to be!
Consider tangling as one of the daily treasures in your life!

There are no mistakes...only opportunities.
We all have those "oops" moments.
Turn them into something positive.

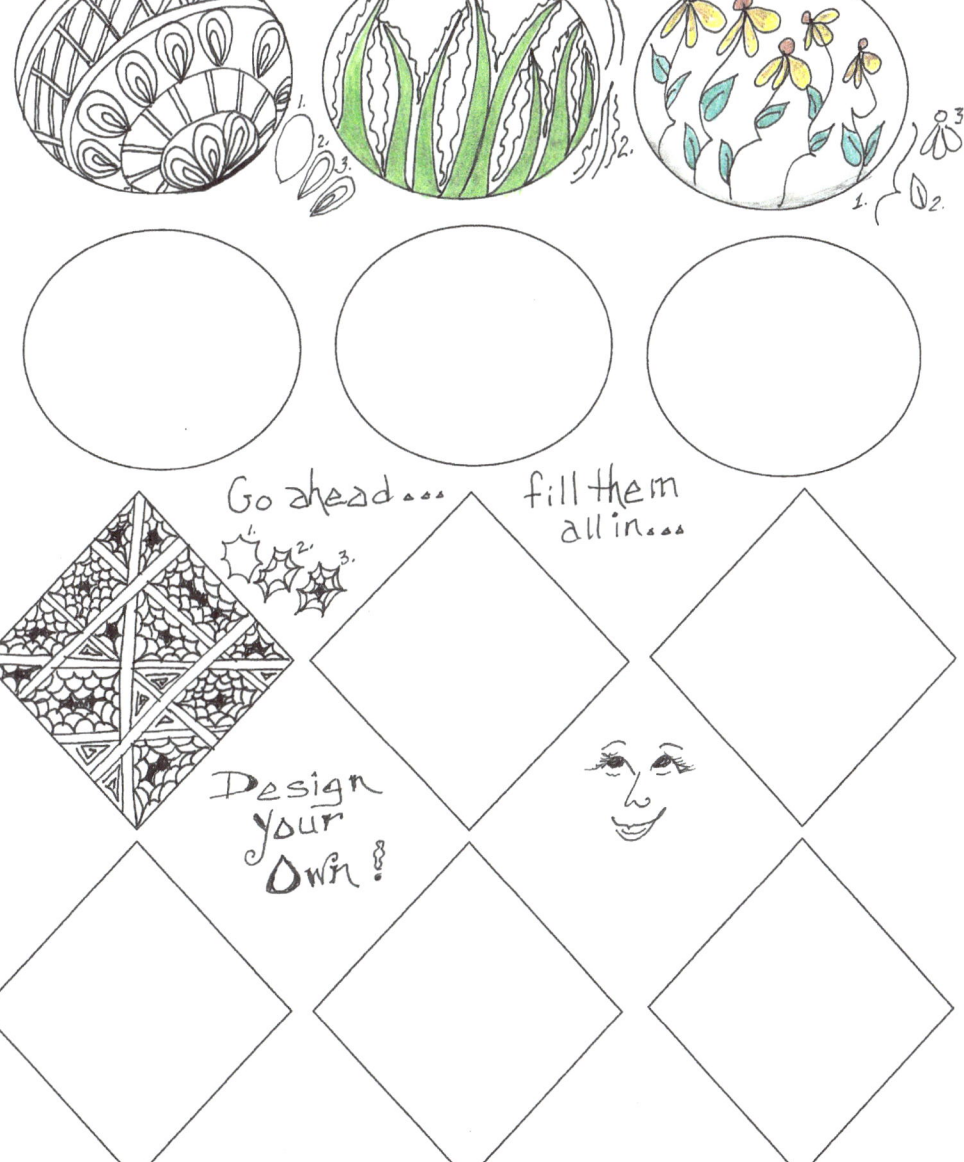

Go ahead...   fill them all in...

Design Your Own!

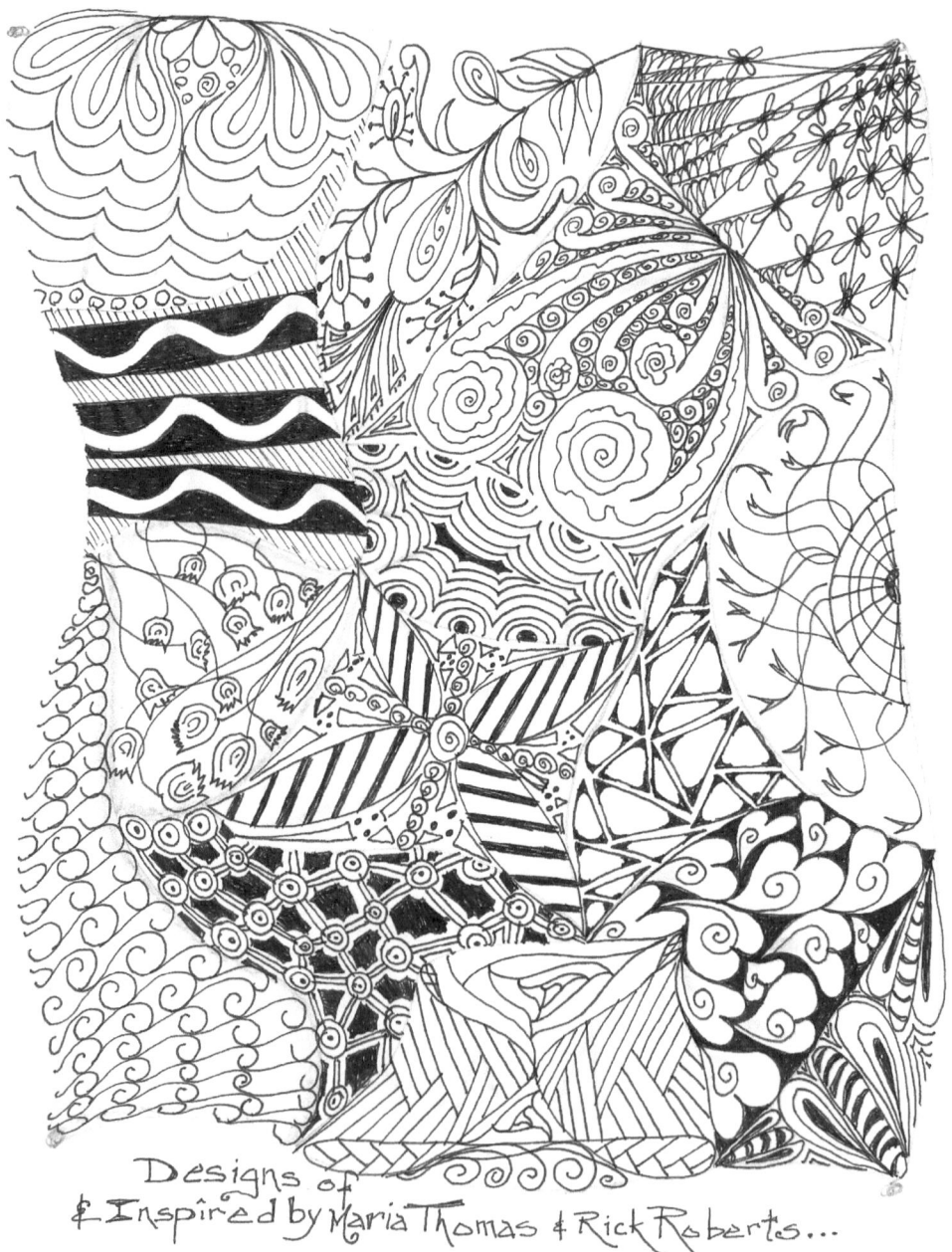

Designs of
& Inspired by Maria Thomas & Rick Roberts...

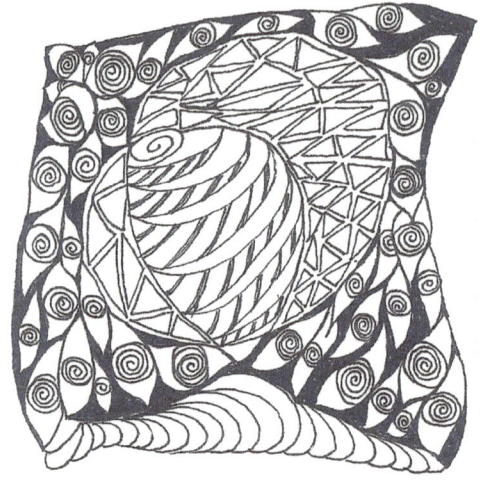

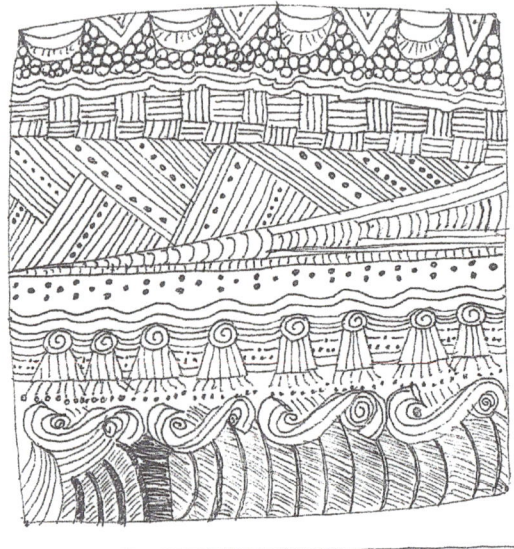

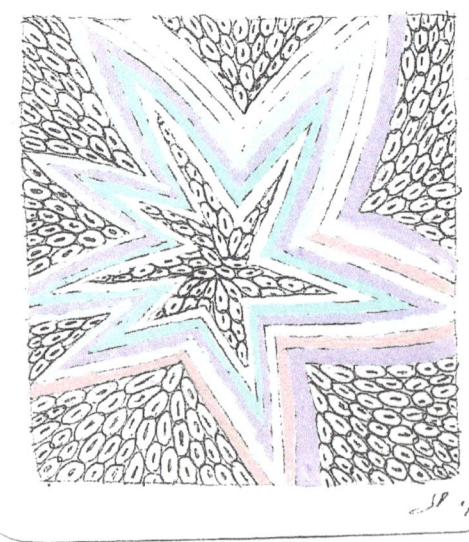

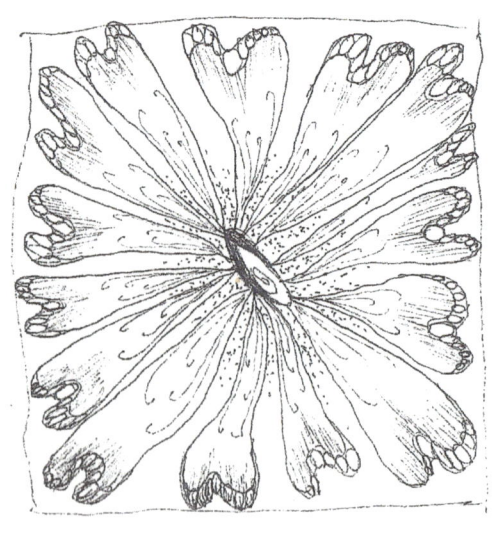

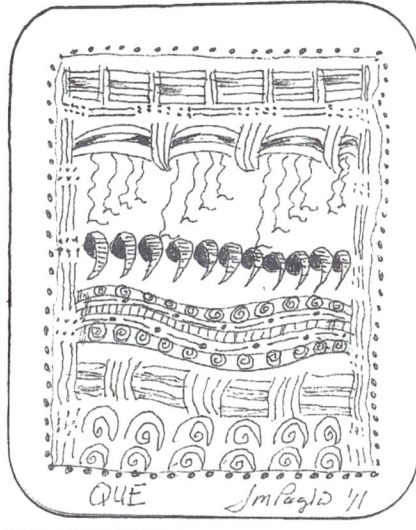

QUE   JmPaglo '11

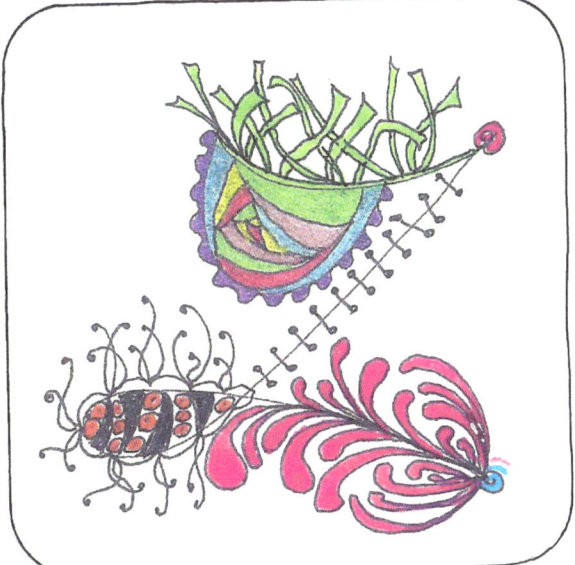

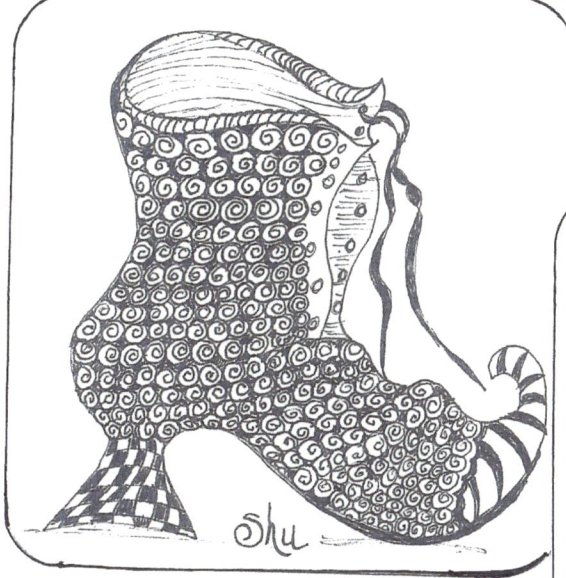

shu

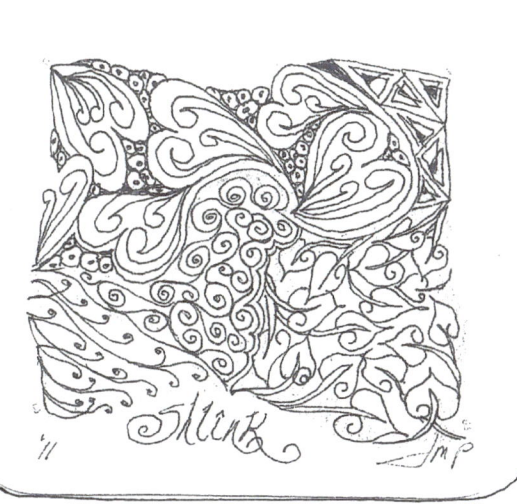

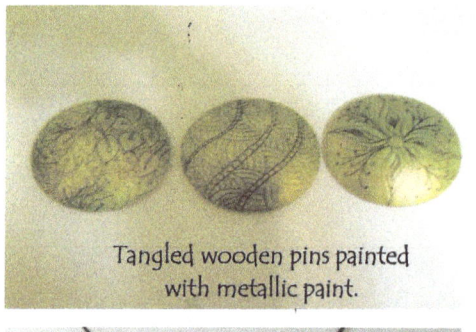

Tangled wooden pins painted
with metallic paint.

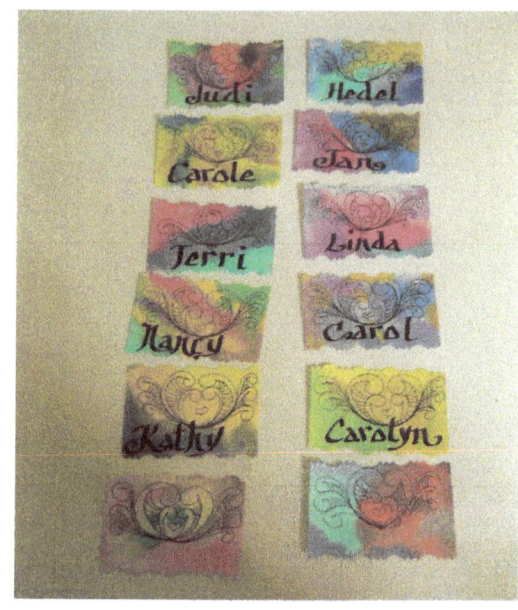

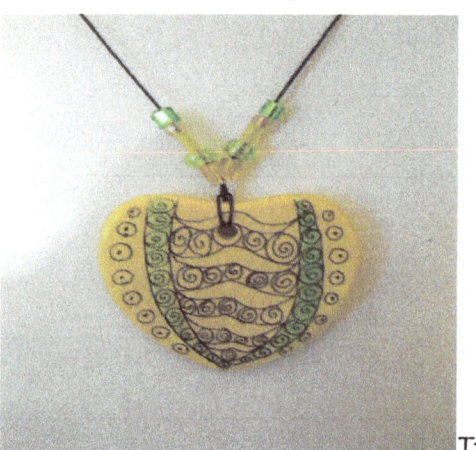

Watercolor Paper Name Tags painted with
Metallic Ink.

Tangled Ceramic
Necklaces

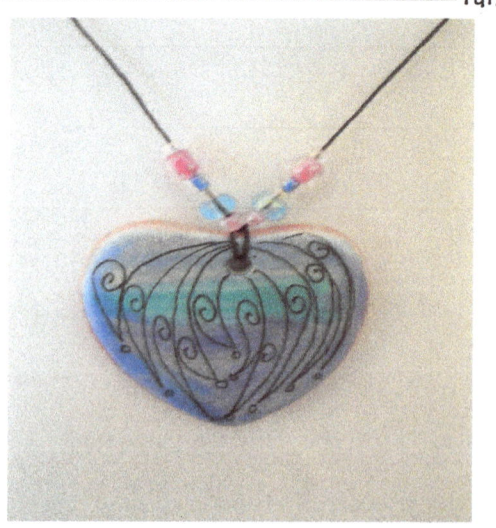

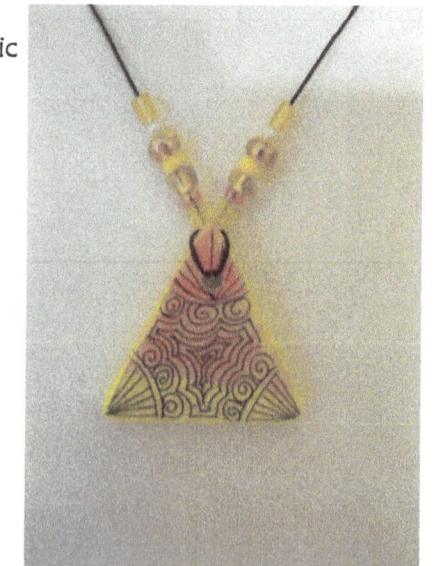

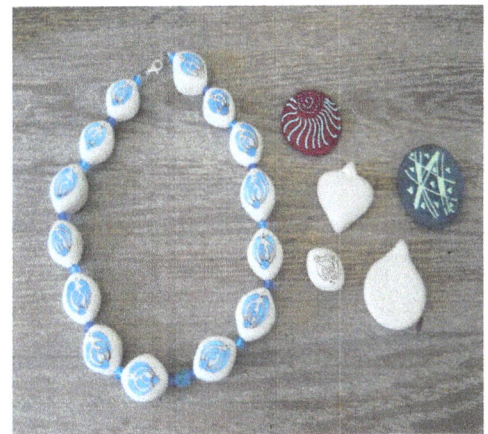

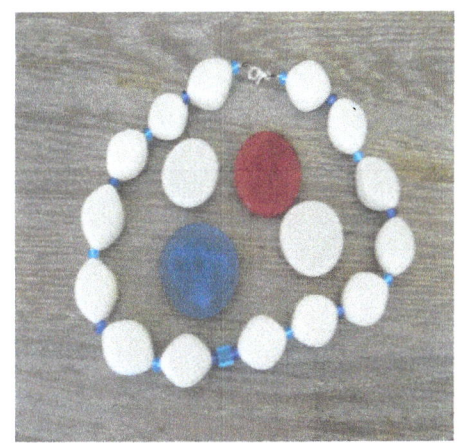

Ceramic Bisque, glass discs, porcelain beads, sea glass…. These are but a few surface suggestions for tangling.

Have some fun with porous surfaces. Begin by sealing them with a multi-purpose sealer, then tangle on them with pens. Dry and spray with a finish. Ta.. Da…

Shrinky Dink Plastic is fun and easy to work with. These two bracelets were designed on the frosted side of the Material before they were baked. Add few seed beads and the project is just delightful.

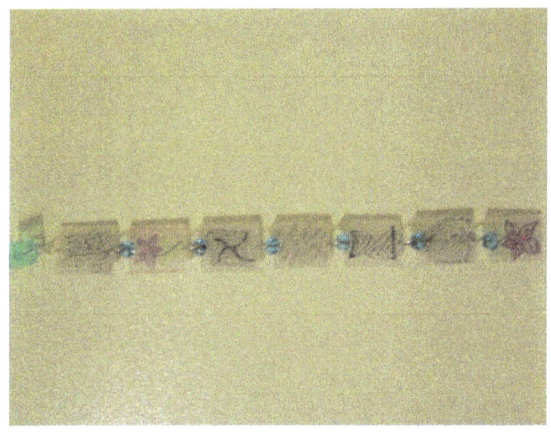

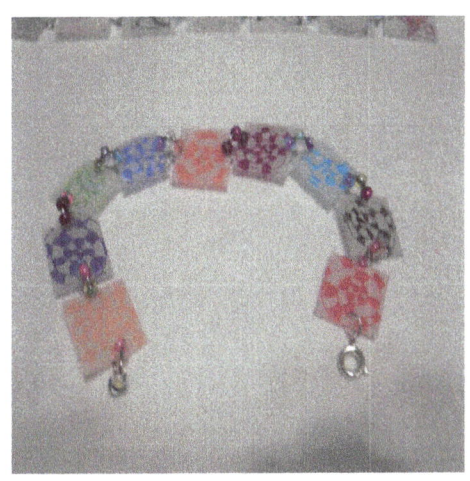

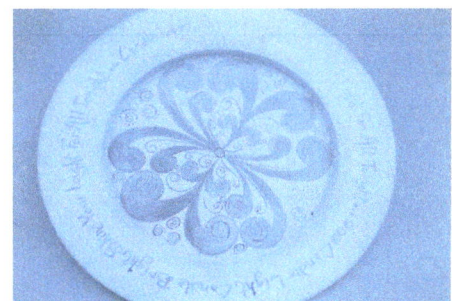

This wooden candle plate was great fun!

Look what I did!
Now you give it a try!!
Go ahead, you can do it....don't be afraid!
Make this YOUR opportunity!

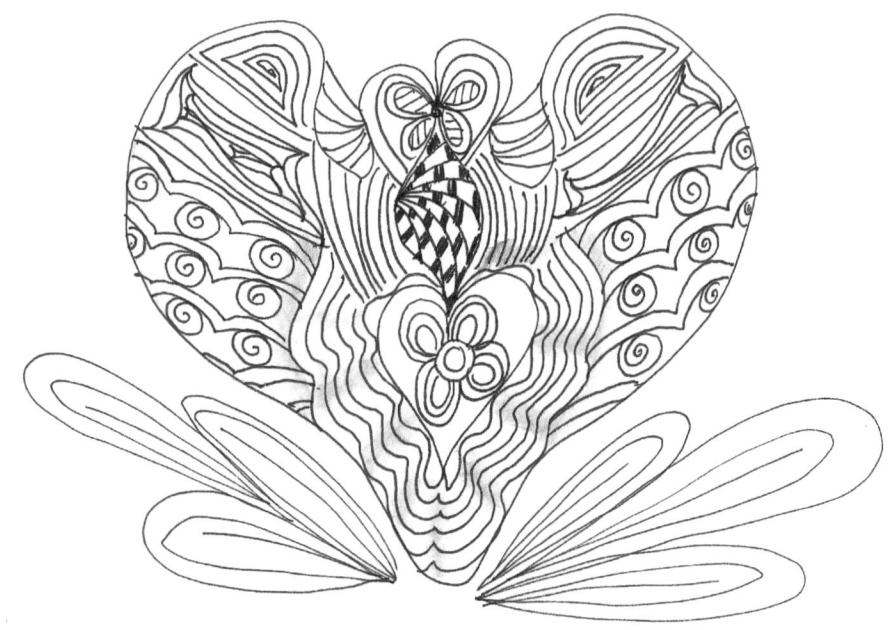

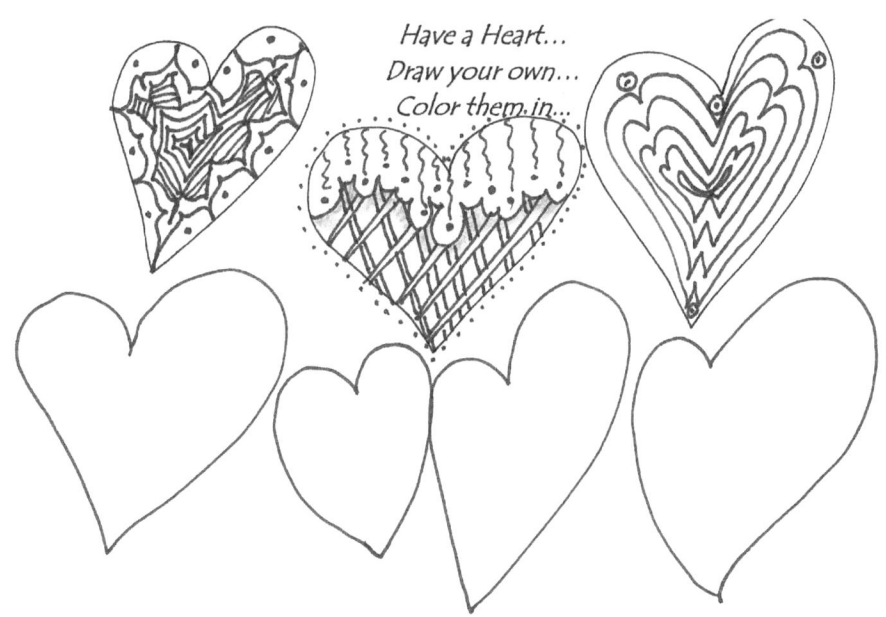

Have a Heart…
Draw your own…
Color them in…

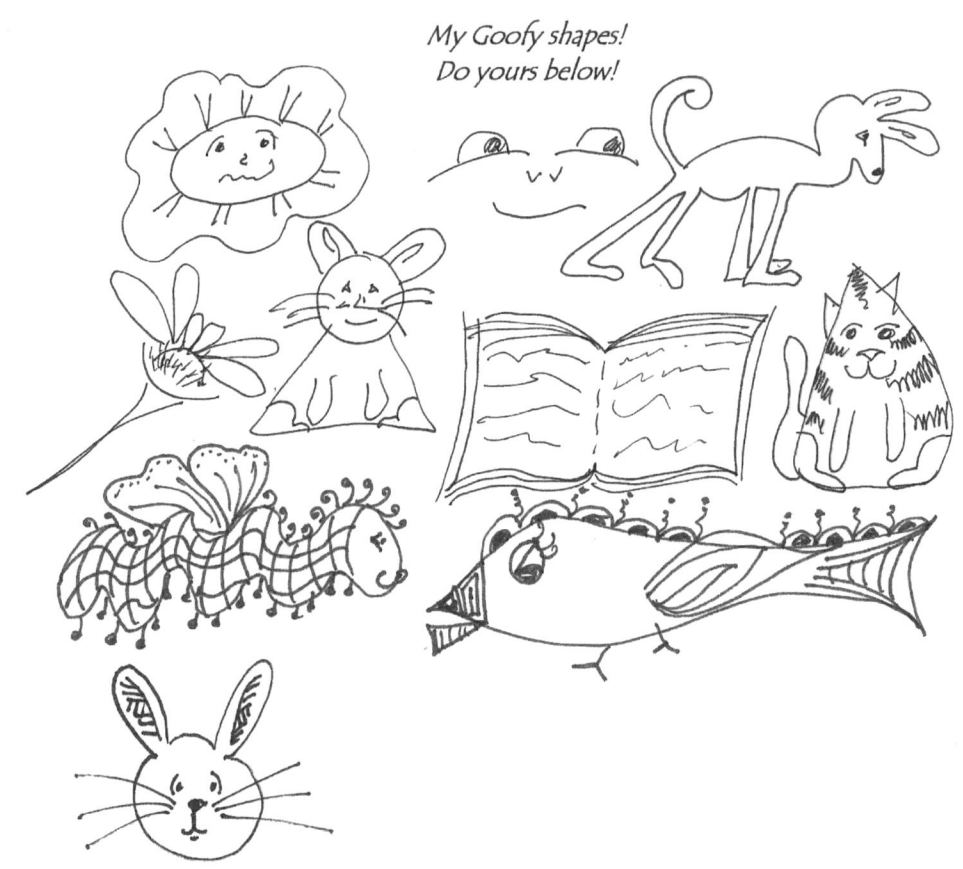

My Goofy shapes!
Do yours below!

Warts with legs!

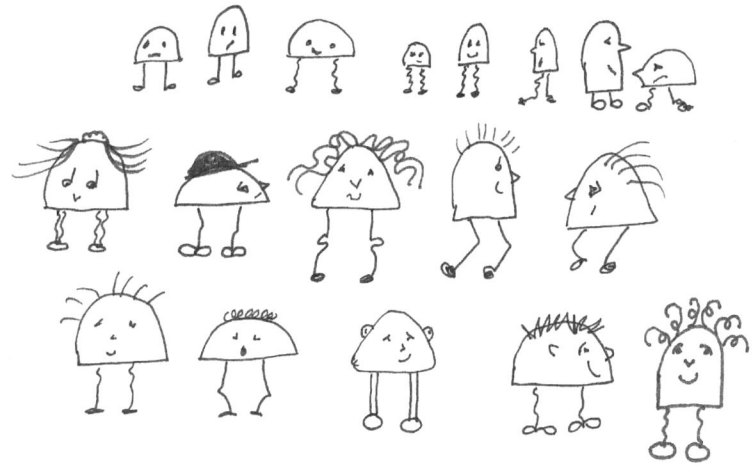

Tomatoes & Potatoes with arms & legs...

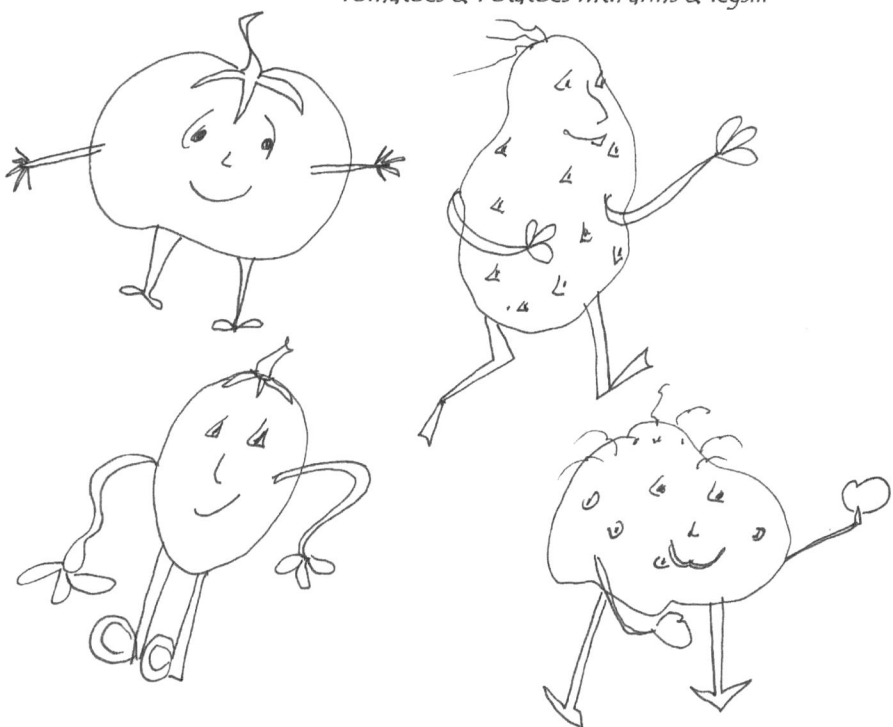

Kooky Kritters!

Bagel Bundle...

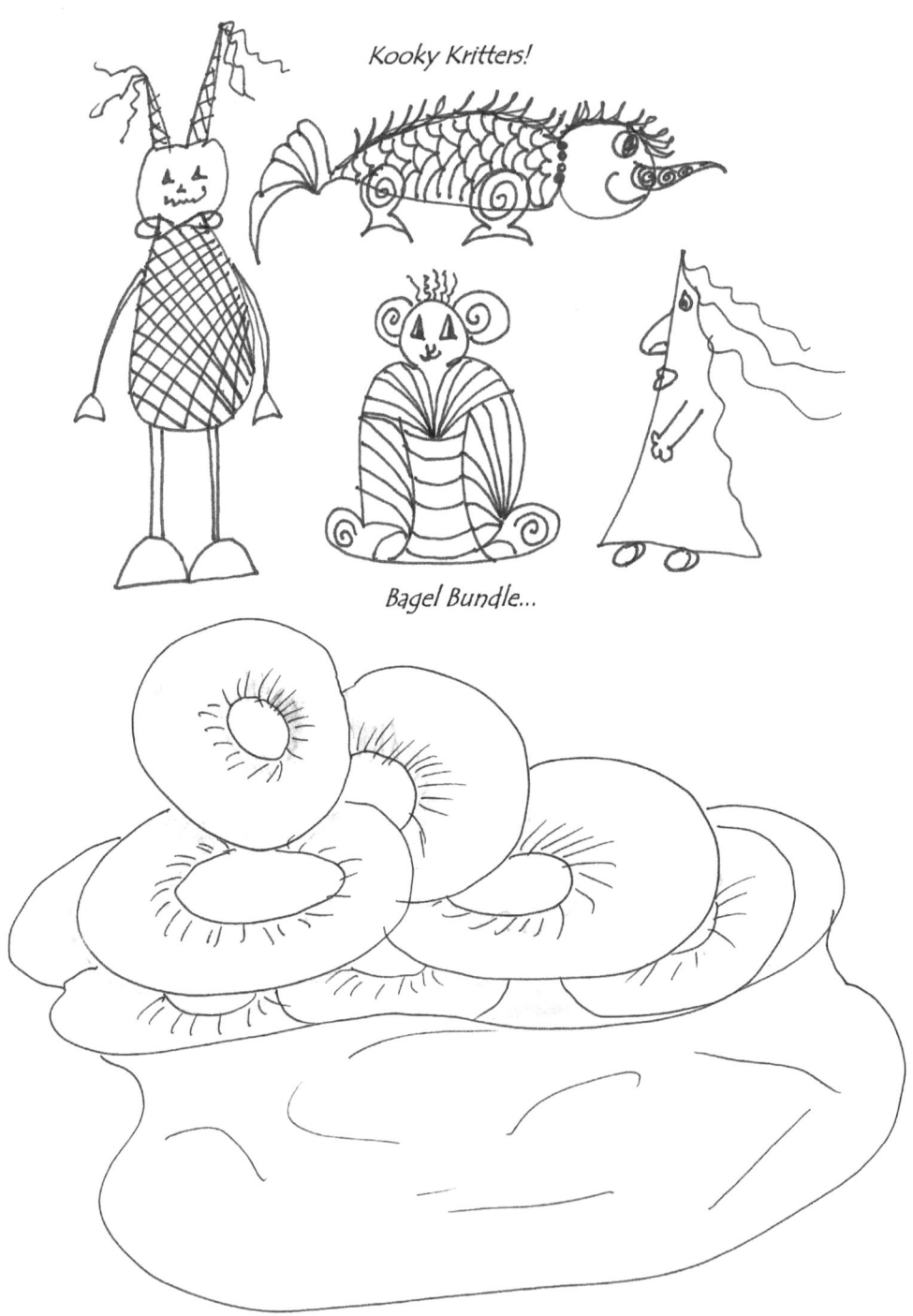

Spindly String beans...

Put yours below...

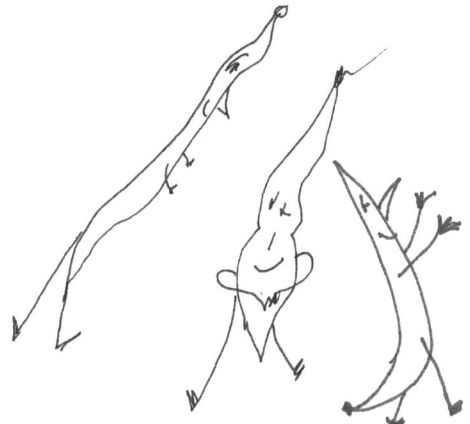

Peppy Peas...

Add your own...

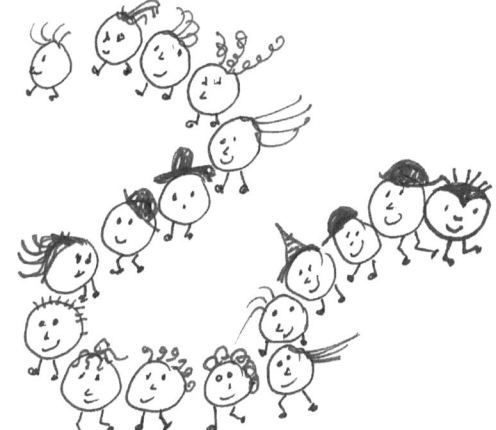

It's time to end this book. It's been great fun sharing my designs with you. I appreciate your interest, and I do hope you have enjoyed yourself. There is no limit to where your tangling journey can and will take you one stroke at a time. Just relax...let your pencil and pen do the work.

As long as I can remember, I have colored, doodled and played with as many surfaces and crayons/markers, etc., as I could get my hands on. As a child at Christmas time, my greatest joy was to open my package of paper and the latest and best Crayola crayons pack that Santa had left for me under the tree. Hours passed on snowy days filled with brisk temperatures. I would lay on the floor in the living room at the lodge where my mother worked, in front of the fireplace and color for hours on end. I wasn't a great one for drawing, but I could doodle with the best of them. (I now know I was a tangler from the start ☺).

Begin your tangling journey if you haven't. There's no time like the present.
Tangle in your journal, while you're on vacation, sitting next to the pool or pond, at the doctor's office, at lunch, while dinner is cooking, or with the kids (yours or someone else's). Every age is a good age for tangling as long as you can hold a pen. Fear is for sissy's, be brave, go for it, take the golden opportunity offered to everyone by stepping outside your comfort zone. Relax, Reflect, Renew, Replenish and Reveal the artist within you.

Enjoy the tranquility this art form can bring into your life. I've never been one for Yoga (or much relaxation/exercise really ☺), but tangling has opened a whole new aspect to my life. I've had many of those "oops" moments, but now I make them into something positive.

Get out your pencil, pen, and blending stump (I call it a "smoocher"), a 3 1/2" x 3 1/2" paper tile and start your journey. Add some color and step back to view the path you have chosen to wander.

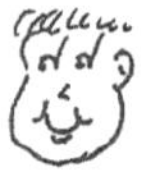

Best regards and keep going...

Jeanne ♪

www.zenoftangling.blogspot.com
www.decorativeartistry.us

Watch for my next two books:

Tangled Letters, Numbers & More... Oh, my

Tangled Baubles, Bangles & Beads

Due date: September/October 2011

Available at www.amazon.com

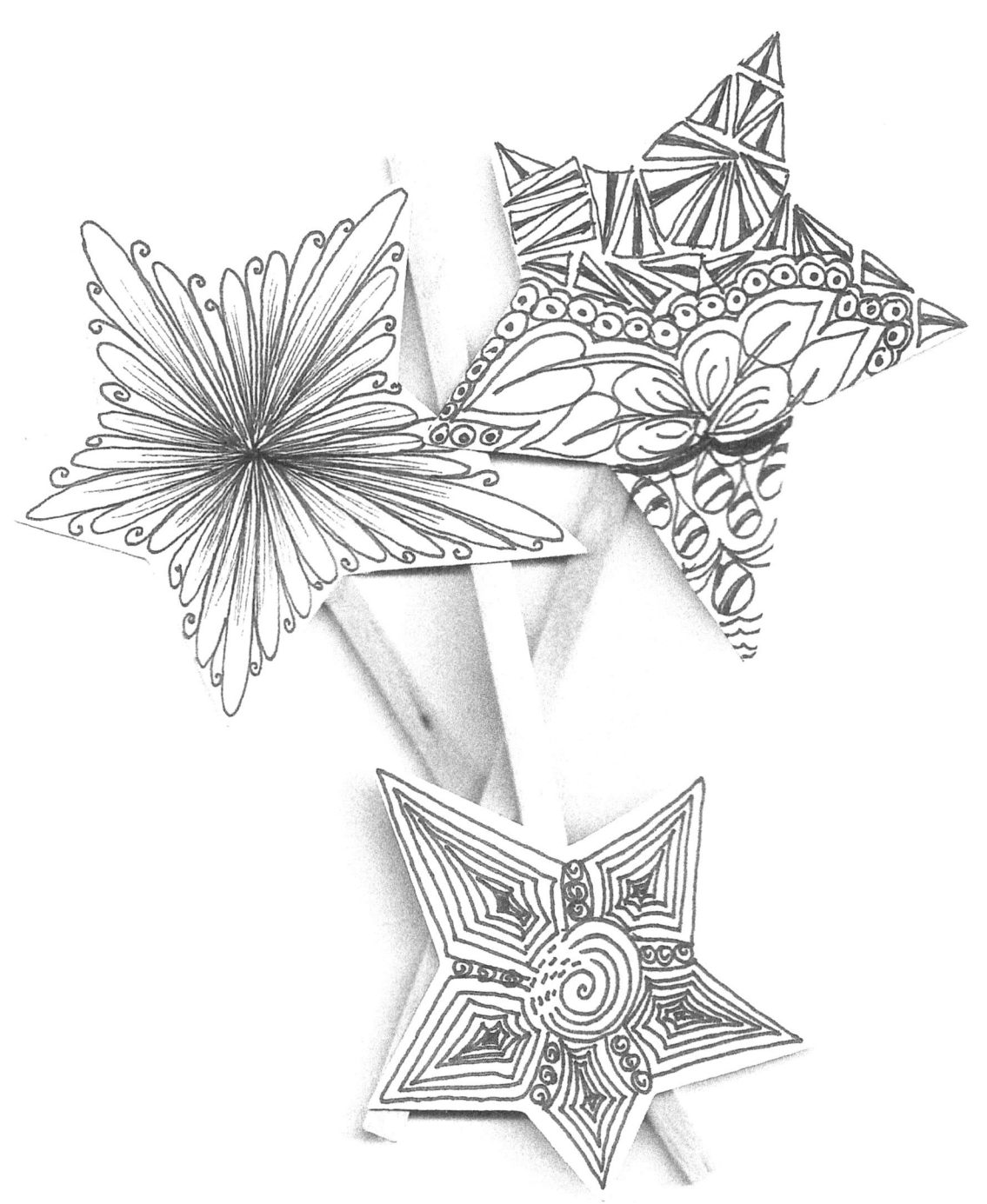